THE
SPIRITUAL
G⬤LFER

Robert "Lumpy" Lumpkin

Library Tales Publishing

LIBRARY TALES PUBLISHING, INC.
244 5TH AVENUE #Q222, NEW YORK, NY, 10001
1-800-754-5016 | 1-347-394-2629
WWW.LIBRARYTALESPUBLISHING.COM

THE SPIRITUAL GOLFER

Published by:
Library Tales Publishing, Inc.
244 5th Avenue, Suite Q222
New York, NY 10001
www.LibraryTalesPublishing.com

For general information on our other products and services, please contact our Customer Care Department at 1-800-754-5016, or fax 917-463-0892. For technical support, please visit www.librarytalespublishing.com

Library Tales Publishing also publishes its books in a variety of electronic formats.
Every content that appears in print is available in electronic books.

ISBN-13: 978-0615568225
ISBN-10: 061556822X

STUDENTS COMMENTS

"Lumpy is a great instructor with an enormous amount of patience and talent. I have read with great pleasure the comments of his students and he always receives the highest performance evaluations. We are fortunate to have Lumpy and his Getaway Golf Academy here at Black Bear Golf Club."

Patrick W., General Manager, Member PGA

"After trying two other golf academies, I tried one more and was lucky to get Lumpy as the instructor. He was able to break down the fundamentals in terms that I could execute & made golf fun again. Mr. Lumpkin changed my golf game from aggravation to appreciation."

Tim G., 28 hdcp to 12 hdcp

"What a pleasure to watch Lumpy swing. I try to emulate his smooth powerful swing. He's always a gentleman and willing to help us struggling amateurs. If you need help with your game, get lessons from Lumpy right away. Thanks for everything Lumpy!"

Jim M., Golf Channel Amateur Tour Player hdcp 16

"Talk about change in my game. When I went to Lumpy I was skeptical because of other lessons I have taken. I am elated that I decided to have Lumpy help me with my swing and my clubs. I'm working with him for my big match in Sept. Thank you Lumpy."

Steve L., 36 hdcp to 24 hdcp

STUDENTS COMMENTS

"I'm no stranger to golf instructors. They all told me the same thing. Why would you want to change your swing? So I went to Lumpy with reservations. One of the best decisions I have made in golf. I just came off a par 72 round and just striped the ball. Lumpy's knowledge and ability to analyze a golf swing is superior. Thanks, Lumpy, I will be back!"

Steve E., Golf Channel Amateur Tour Player hdcp 4

"Lumpy has an eye for the golf swing. We're playing a practice round and he saw my left hip was not clearing. He yanked my pocket around, and presto, just like magic I started ripping the driver. Yep, an exciting moment, on the 9th hole I out drove Lumpy with my 325 yard blast. He has helped me for years and is a great Professional Player & Instructor."

Richard H., Former Professional Tour Player hdcp 4

"Before working with Lumpy I was a 40 hdcp & had decided to quit golfing. With his help I'm now a 12 hdcp & can't play enough. He is a very knowledgeable & patient teacher who doesn't force a cookie cutter approach, but rather provides a customized method to build a swing that fits your personal style & comfort level. I highly recommend Lumpy!"

Kevin M., Golf Channel Amateur Tour Player hdcp 12

Robert "Lumpy" Lumpkin is very unique in his ability to quickly evaluate a golf swing, and to immediately judge the suitability of the clubs the player is using. Lumpy is nothing less than a genius at custom fitting and building clubs, helping his students improve even faster.

Alvin Cloyd, Master Club Builder, Al's Custom Golf

ABOUT THE BOOK

Abiding deep within every golfer's spirit is a natural swing. After more than twenty years of teaching golfers of all levels and playing rounds of golf with his students, Lumpy knew he had to find a way to help golfers hit those great golf shots they were capable of hitting. The secrets that he has shared with his students are now revealed in this exciting new book.

INTRODUCTION

In sharing my thoughts and experiences, it is my sincere wish that golfers of all skill levels will be able to take something away that will improve their ability to play the game of golf.

Not all of any book's contents apply to all golfers, so read and enjoy this book and apply those things that will help you in your quest to be a better golfer.

I would like to thank all my students from over the years for a memorable journey. To all the golfers I have had the pleasure to teach and play golf with, thank you. For those of you that recognize your funny stories, may I express to you an extra portion of thanks for helping keep golf so much fun!

And finally, I have tried to recognize and give credit to all those that have taught me, and from whom I have studied and learned. If I have been remiss in any of these areas, please accept my apology, for that was not my intent.

I have been so blessed to have met, learned and played golf with some of the best players to have ever played this game. To all of you, I wish the continued success you so richly deserve.

Now let's tee up and find that great golfer inside you, and the natural swing that abides deep within your spirit!

CHAPTER 1
THE NATURAL GOLF SWING INSIDE YOU

The question of how to play great golf has been asked for decades upon decades. Golf ranges and courses are littered with broken souls. Golfers around the world have seen themselves hit a great golf shot and wonder in amazement as to just how easy it seemed to have happened, only to be plunged back to earth in despair when not able to repeat those great shots consistently.

As a golfer, have you ever hit a really bad shot out of bounds or in the water? If you have ever teed it up on a golf course, we know the answer is yes. You probably have also thrown a ball down in disgust and, just like magic, hit a perfect shot! This begs the question: WHY was the second shot great?

To find that answer, we will talk about the great Tiger Woods, as well as some of the other great golfers, for many of the same attributes bless them all. Whether you are one of Tiger's many fans or not, most golfers will agree that he is one of the greatest players to have ever played the game of golf. Who are some of the other greatest players of all time? Well let's narrow it down to the only players to win all four modern major events in their careers, meaning the Masters, U. S. Open, British Open, and PGA. There are only five: Ben Hogan, Gene Sarazen, Gary Player, Jack Nicklaus and Tiger Woods.

We would be remiss not to include the greatest amateur of all time, and some say the greatest player period, the incomparable Bobby Jones. He won what is referred to as the Grand Slam of Golf. Mr. Jones won the U. S. Amateur, U. S. Open, British Amateur and the

British Open, all in the same year of competition! Mr. Jones never played professional golf and always believed that golf should be played for fun and for the chance of excelling in competition.

There are, of course, many great players who did not win all four of the modern majors, or any for that matter, so it should be pointed out that the fact that this focus does not include these players in no way lessens their great accomplishments. Also, there are indeed many great women golfers in our history, and they are hereby acknowledged and appreciated. Point in fact: I could have devoted an entire book to these great lady golfers.

So golf fans, because of the many great players in the world, we know you have a favorite or two that you enjoy watching on TV, whether a "young gun", "lady" or a "senior". Please continue to watch, enjoy, and learn from these great players.

How on God's green earth does this apply to you, the golfer? Golf's greatness _is_ in you, and it simply means there is a unique golf swing inside each and every one of us. It abides deep within our spirit. The question is: How do you bring it out and hit those magically perfect shots?

Let us first explain the categories of golfers, how greatness is judged in each, and then you determine which category you fit into.

The professional golfer category is reserved for those golfers who play the game on tour for money and winning tournaments. Greatness is easy to determine because you win money, tournaments or both. Also, in this category, you are judged by which tournaments you win, with the modern major events taking center stage.

The golf professional category is reserved for those golfers who manage golf facilities. Greatness is judged by how financially successful the golf facilities are and thereby, how much the golf professional earns.

The professional golf instructor category is reserved for those golfers who make a living teaching the game of golf. Greatness is judged by how successfully he or she is able to help golfers improve their golf game in both scores and enjoyment.

The competitive amateur golfer category is reserved for those golfers who love winning golf tournaments for just the love of the game and competition. Greatness is defined by winning golf tournaments. These golfers, however, have no desire to try to make a living in the game of golf...at least not yet.

The recreational amateur golfer category is reserved for those golfers who love to play the game of golf as a fun sport. Greatness is judged by beating their best scoring round, playing the game to the best of their abilities, always striving to improve, winning the weekend Nassau bet against their playing partners, making that career golf shot, (with witnesses), knowing that they have just hit a shot that even the "TV Pros" would be proud of, and of course, bragging rights in the pub after play.

I have had the great fortune to be included in each of the categories, though I must confess I never made the "Big Show", in category one. I have, however, spent more than twenty years in category three, a professional golf instructor.

The main focus of this book is for all golfers everywhere who fall into the last two categories. And you can be proud to be in these categories! After all, you are in good company, as these categories contains 98% of all golfers worldwide. And while we are speaking of golfers worldwide, did you know that the average golfer's score, according to the USGA[17] scoring system, is approximately 98?

Why do I mention the average score? If you will apply what you learn in this book, there is no reason for you not to improve your game dramatically. That's right. If you have never broken 100, or 90 or 80, you will be able to now.

What is it about Tiger and the great players that the recreational golfer is missing?

We will look at the obvious that is written about ad infinitum. Besides talent, practice, coaching, fitness, mental toughness, great golf swing, great putting, great chipping, great imagination, great support, the will to win and hours upon hours of dedication, there is <u>most importantly</u> this fact:

*They have learned **not to fight** the natural swing inside them.*

Oh come on, it can't be that simple, you say! Well, ask yourself this question: Do Tiger Woods, Jack Nicklaus, Ben Hogan, Gene Sarazen, Gary Player and Bobby Jones swings all look alike? For fun, let's add to this list Arnold Palmer, Jim Furyk, Phil Mickelson, Peter Jacobsen, Bob Murphy, Nancy Lopez, Natalie Gulbis, Tom Kite, Tom Watson, Chi Chi Rodriguez, and Lee Trevino.

Watch these great players' swing, and you will agree they are all very unique. However, their swings have three physical things in common, and we will cover what they are and how you can duplicate them with your own natural swing. While I have not ever had the pleasure to speak with Tiger, other than saying hello to him at the 2005 President's Cup, I have studied his game. Same goes for Jack Nicklaus.

Having had the pleasure of teaching amateurs and professionals at all levels, the one common theme that always emerges is that when golfers find their natural swing inside them, they improve dramatically. This improvement is almost immediate.

So, why then, is this not written about and covered in the normal golf instruction magazines? Well, it is written about and the great players are intimately knowledgeable of the ramifications of "not trusting your natural swing inside you." Dr. Bob Rotella[5], noted sports psychologist, works with many of the great golfers. Dr. Rotella's mental approach to the game includes 'giving up control to gain control'. Now, while I do not pretend to be a psychologist, if one studies his findings as well as other noted psychologists, such as Dr. Lewis Smith[7], one cannot help but begin to see the logic of just trusting your natural swing *that is* inside you.

Some mechanical golf swing teachers prefer to look at it this way: Why spend hours of practice building a golf swing that you can trust, and then not use it on the golf course when you play? This all boils down to saying the same thing, trust your golf swing *that is* inside you. All golfers naturally have timing, rhythm and tempo that is unique to them. The secret is to find it and use it.

Now here is where your exciting journey begins. To find the natural golf swing inside you, first go back to the shot you hit in disgust. You see, what happened was that you gave no thought as to how to hit that shot. You just swung. This is worth repeating: you gave no thought as to how to hit the shot and just swung. This naturally created another phenomenon. You also gave no thought to the results!

When you learn to accept the results, whether good or bad, pressure drains from your body like water flowing over the Hoover Dam. Pressure does strange things to our bodies. One of those things is interfering with our natural abilities. A great example that has been used many times is this: If we place a balance beam, which is only four inches wide, on the floor and ask you to walk across it, 99.9% of all golfers would have no trouble whatsoever not falling off. But if we raise that beam twenty feet in the air, look out; you better have a safety net. The reason this occurs is because the mind begins to think about the results, and in most cases how badly we would be hurt if we fall off the beam, or in a single word…FEAR!

You have just learned one of the secrets of the great golfers. They conquer the fear of hitting a bad shot. They knocked fear out! That is exactly what you did when you <u>just</u> threw the ball down and <u>just</u> swung.

Let's take a deeper look at fear, because playing golf and life have their parallels. It's probably accurate to say that most people dream of being their own boss. Speaking from personal experience, you must conquer the fear of failure, or the fear of success to even venture in that direction. I have had my share of both successes and failures in business ventures and golf.

But alas, the only way to get experience is to plunge in and learn from those failures and successes. There are, of course, different kinds of fear. Take the person who has panic attacks when appearing in front of a group of people. As a public speaker before golf groups and organizations, I'm familiar with the nervousness that people experience. Fortunately, this fear is usually related to the fear of failure: What will they think? Will I misspeak? Will they like me and what I have to say? I say fortunately, because being well prepared is the easiest way to overcome the fear that may emerge as the time approaches for your introduction. Ah, life's parallel, being well prepared on the first tee in front of your playing group, which we will get to in the next chapter.

While working part-time at a golf course in my twenties, and still serving in the U. S. Army Security Agency, I felt that the Big Tour was within my grasp. However, I listened to a supposed friend, who told me I was too old to make the tour. Sad that I listened and believed him, isn't it?

As a result of working part-time at that golf course, and while helping some golfers improve their games, they revealed that they were police officers and began to recruit me. They were successful in their efforts, and after my military discharge, I served the community for five years in law enforcement. The point to all of this, is that fear takes many forms. Facing life and death situations can put other of life's fears in perspective. So, in my case, having served in the Army and as a police officer, I am able to draw upon those fearful encounters to assist me in whatever the endeavor is that I am undertaking. Trust me when I tell you this, you can overcome whatever fear that may present itself, in whatever form it may come.

In golf, this means you can conquer any fear that raises its ugly head and leap to the top of the leaderboard!

LEADERS

HOLE	1	2	3	4	5	6	7	8	9
PAR	4	4	3	5	4	4	3	4	5
YOUR NAME	3	4	3	4	4	3	2	4	4
WOODS	4	4	2	3	4	4	3	4	6
MICHELSON	4	4	4	4	4	3	3	4	4
STRICKER	4	4	3	4	4	4	3	4	5
GARCIA	5	3	3	5	4	4	2	5	5

[5]Dr. Bob Rotella, sports psychologist (Books and tapes are available in book stores and online)

[7]Dr. Lewis Smith, Golf Control, Inc 17177 N. Laurel Park Drive, Suite 205, Livonia, Michigan

NOTES

~~~~~~~~~~~~~~~~~~~~

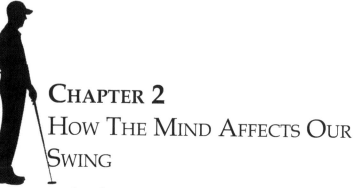

CHAPTER 2
HOW THE MIND AFFECTS OUR SWING

Let's now examine the second mental aspect of the game that great players master. Ever go to a professional golf tournament or watch it closely on TV? Notice how close the fans are to the action. This is unique in all of sports. You, the fan, can be right next to these great athletes; so close that you are able to give them a high five and receive one in return.

Notice how close the fans are on the tee box when the players tee off? Ever wonder if you could hit a shot with people so close to the flight of the ball?

If you have had the good fortune of playing in a pro-am, you have probably gotten a small taste of the "nerves on edge" as you teed off. If not, just picture yourself teeing off with all those people *seemingly right in the line of fire*. WOW!

The great players accept whatever the environment is as a naturally occurring event. They welcome and enjoy it. No matter that there are thousands of fans closely watching their every move. No matter that they are teeing off over a side of the ocean or a two hundred and fifty yard carry over a tormenting patch of cactus and desert. No matter that there are hundreds of media types all over the course to catch every mistake for the whole world to see and cringe over.

Golf course designers often intentionally place objects and natural terrain in the line of fire to make the hole look more intimidating. These features also serve to get the player to think strategy. But, it is all part of the beautiful aesthetics that we get to enjoy playing magnificent golf courses.

© Photo edited by
Robert "Lumpy" Lumpkin

You may be thinking, yeah, but I don't have to play in front of fans or a TV audience, so how does this apply to me, the recreational golfer? Please understand that your fellow golfers in your foursome can be just as intimidating as a gallery of fans, if you let them.

Picture for a moment you with your weekend foursome. You are waiting to tee off on the first tee. You look over and see one of your playing partners warming up his swing. He is swinging at old pine cones, leaves or perhaps an old cigarette butt. Notice how smooth and natural his swing looks.

Now picture him as he tees the ball up and makes his first swing of the day. Oh my, the swing did not look anything like the practice swing at the pine cone, did it? Yeah, I got ya. You probably do the same thing. But do not despair! Instead, let's look at why that occurs.

First of all, you have not accepted the environment. You are worried about what your buddies are going to think if you hit a bad shot. Secondly, you have not conquered the fear of hitting a bad shot, so you are thinking about how to make the swing and hit the ball. Thoughts go racing through your mind. Keep the left arm straight, head steady, don't sway, make sure to make a shoulder turn, don't hit it out of bounds, etc., and all of a sudden, you've hit a bad shot. Sound familiar?

Now, let's picture a different scenario. You get to hit as many balls off the tee as you want until you have hit the shot you are happy with and you only have to count one stroke. You have just learned how pressure affects your swing, and thereby, the results. Can you imagine the difference?

Question is: How do we accept the environment and not worry about hitting a bad shot? Believe this as an absolute fact: Your playing partners are too worried about their own golf shot to give what you do a second thought. Also, know this: There is nothing they can do to help or hurt your chances of hitting a great shot, and most importantly, so what if you hit a bad shot? Is it going to make or break your day or define your round of golf?

Now, before you think this is too critical of the recreational golfer, let me share a true story of my own experience. While playing in a professional tour event, on the first tee I literally topped the ball into a lake right in front of the tee box. Yes, it was embarrassing to say the least, but we all make bad golf shots!

Since I was the last of the pros to tee off for that tee time, I immediately made a joke with a real big smile about "getting my monies worth on that one," as I re-teed another ball. I made the joke to relax and get my focus on just swinging. I ripped the next ball down the middle over 300 yards, hit the next shot on the green about 20 feet right of the pin, and knocked in the putt for a great bogey. My final score was not great, a 75, but had I let that first shot determine my round of golf, the score could have been a total disaster.

Being most fortunate to have been taught golf by the late Tom Furgason, who shared with me that he once served as a shag caddy for Ben Hogan, I learned that all pros hit bad shots. It has been said that when Ben Hogan shot a 68 he felt he only hit 4 perfect shots in the round. Whoa! Whether that is true or not, it does drive the point home. We are clearly going to have more controlled misses than we are going to have perfect shots, and we are going to have our share of bad shots in our round of golf. How you handle those miss hit and bad shots plays a huge role in your final score.

Now, an examination of what physically occurs in the example on the first tee. Instead of just swinging like we did at the pine cone, we change to trying to hit the ball and make the shot that we desire. Get this ingrained in your mind forever and ever: Just brush the grass and…**"The ball simply gets in the way of the swing."** Just as the pine cone got in the way of our swing when we warmed up, that is exactly the way we want to swing when we make a pass with the ball in the way.

"The best judge of the golf swing is the flight of the ball." Again, a quote attributed to Ben Hogan. In laymen's terms, just swing your natural swing that's inside you and let the club do the work. Just brush the grass and…**"The ball simply gets in the way of the swing."**

Now, let's look at the third mental aspect that the great players master. Ever notice how smooth and effortless their swings appear? It does not matter that they all look different; the timing, rhythm and tempo is an artistic thing of beauty.

Timing, rhythm and tempo reveal the natural physical action being undertaken in the golf swing. Broken down, it is the natural coordination of the action of swinging an object as quickly as possible, while not over extending one's ability to maintain proper balance. In other words: one does not try to hit the ball, but rather focuses on the swinging of the club without trying to make the ball go further than one's natural ability.

For the best way to understand and practice your timing, rhythm and tempo, I highly recommend the book and CD: Tour Tempo[9]. This has the tempo of several famous tour players on it and you can learn how your tempo compares to your favorite tour player. This is a great way to listen to the tempo, either to a metronome type sound or to words.

Not a believer? Alright, try this yourself. Ever how far you normally hit a five iron, add 30 yards and try to hit it that far. Now try to hit it 20 yards less than you normally do. What happens when you try to hit the ball 30 yards further? What happens when you try to hit the ball 20 yards shorter?

If you are like most golfers, the swing becomes a violent out of control effort to try to hit the ball 30 yards further, but the swing becomes smooth, effortless and graceful when you try to hit the ball 20 yards shorter. This is what great players learn, and why some players do not hit the ball as far as others. They learned to swing within themselves!

One of my personal favorite golfers to watch is Fred Funk. Of course Fred is never going to hit the ball as far as Tiger, and his swing would become an out of control violent action if he even tried.

Having said this, there is a way to gain more distance within your own natural swing, which we will cover later. (A few hints here are: flexibility, golf muscle strength (and I don't mean you need to become a body builder), inside swing path, properly fitted clubs, and most importantly, proper impact position).

Now, how do we get that proper timing, rhythm, and tempo? First, we must accept the fact that we remember by pictures. To prove this, if I ask you what an elephant is, what is the first thing that comes into your mind? That's right, you picture an elephant. Or if I say giraffe, you see a giraffe. Because we remember in pictures, I have included pictures in every chapter.

So when I say what a perfectly smooth golf swing looks like, you probably picture Ernie Els, Fred Couples, Davis Love III, or other players from our golf history such as Bobby Jones, Sam Snead or Payne Stewart. If you have another favorite, that's fine too. If you did not picture one in your mind, any one of the golfers mentioned would be great.

The important thing is to find one of the great swingers of the golf club and learn all you can by watching what they do. When you practice your golf swing, it is important to try and feel like they look, 'in your mind's eye'. Now not that I consider myself in the league of these great players, the following stop action photos of my swing can help give you the mental images. In the next chapter, we will take an in-depth view of each of the positions.

PROPER SWING POSITIONS

A recreational golfer and friend of mine, who is about an 18 handicap, often tells other golfers that my swing is so smooth and effortless that he does not understand how I am able to hit the ball so far. I only mention this because it is one the greatest compliments a professional golfer can receive about their swing, and to help convince you that not only do I advocate what is being related in this book, but that it works.

As we slowly begin evolving into how the mind affects our physical ability, our golf striking ability improves. I am not naïve and believe that just changing your mind is going to change your golf ball striking ability into a tour pro. To my knowledge, no golf ball has ever been struck by the mind. However, great players learn how to control their minds, thus enhancing the ability to play the game of golf.

With all the information that bombards our minds, it begs the question: How do we put the other thoughts out of our minds in order to focus on playing golf? We see things, hear things and remember things constantly. Our gears are always grinding, trying to solve something that is puzzling us, and suddenly the light bulb goes on with a new idea.

In my experience, you simply prioritize your thoughts. The best way is to write down a schedule of the things that are in your mind. Taking care of the items that you can, before playing golf; is like cleaning out a closet and getting rid of the clutter. For the remaining items, write down a timetable in which you will address them. Then, just relax and enjoy playing golf.

Because our minds can be trained and learn what we teach it, a certain area of our mind does not know what is real or perceived, only what we tell it. In other words, if we were taught that an elephant was a giraffe, then that is what we would picture. Fascinating, isn't it?

So, to get the proper timing, rhythm and tempo, you need to picture one of the great golfers, and see their swing in your mind's eye. See just how smooth, effortless and in balance their swing appears. Then, physically practice swinging your driver, "The Big Dog", like you do not care how far the ball goes; just swinging in balance and smooth. You are going to be surprised at how far you hit the ball, and how accurate. You can swing as fast as you want to, as long as you maintain your balance.

There are so many highlight reels on Tiger's great shots that it could fill a room in the Smithsonian. But, we can also learn from his bad shots. Remember seeing him, on occasion, swing and hit the ball way off line. If you are like most golfers, you were either stunned or just in plain old shock. Now, not to be presumptuous to know Tiger's mind, because after all, to quote one of the great golfers of all time, Johnny Miller, on a national broadcast; and I quote as nearly as I can remember: "If I knew how Tiger thought, I would not be sitting up here in this booth," end quote. However, having qualified that, there is a very good chance that one of the three mental processes that we have discussed broke down. There is also the possibility that Tiger, who like all of us, after all, is human and his body simply did not cooperate. But let's examine what could have happened, within our focus.

Those in review are: "trust your golf swing", "environment acceptance" and "timing, rhythm and tempo". Within each of these fall several items that affect how well you manage them.

Within "trust your golf swing" is focusing on the swing and not the mechanics of how to make the swing, as well as being confident that your swing is going to work, thus the word trust. Failure to believe that the swing will create the shot you have in mind is the same as not trusting.

Within "environment acceptance" is also blocking out any unwanted distractions. You have seen Tiger back away from a shot because of a camera shutter clicking. In that case, it was a failure to either accept it as the environment, or, not able to block it out at that moment, for whatever reason.

Within "timing, rhythm and tempo" is the act of swinging too hard, or trying a swing that you have not gained total confidence in. Tiger could have tried to play a certain shot that he was not fully prepared to play. We have all watched as he rehearses the shot he has in mind that he wants to play. This is something we should all pick up on and incorporate into our routine.

If you have had the pleasure of watching the movie, "Tin Cup", you will no doubt remember two things. One is that when Tin Cup gets the shanks, he makes a statement to the effect: "pro-nation, sub-pro-nation, my God my swing feels like an unfolding lawn chair." That is a great example of not trusting your golf swing. Remember his caddy Romeo's advice. "Put all your change in your left pocket, tie a double knot in your left shoe, turn your visor around backwards and place this tee … behind your left ear." Tin Cup said, "I look like a fool." Romeo said, "What do you think you look like shooting those hot chili peppers up Lee Janzen's ass?"

Tin Cup then proceeds to take out his seven iron and hit a perfect golf shot. Romeo goes on to tell him it's because he is not thinking about hitting the shot, his girlfriend, or anything else, and is just letting his golf swing go naturally. What great advice!

The other great thing you will remember is the twelve he makes on the final hole of the U. S. Open. Being convinced that he can knock it on the green in two; he proceeds to hit five balls in the water. Dropping his last ball he has in his bag, he is determined to hit it on the green, even though if this ball goes in the water, he will be disqualified because he cannot finish the hole and turn in a scorecard. Yep, he makes the swing, and the ball carries the water and goes in the hole for a smooth twelve. This is a great example of trusting your golf swing, but a horrible example of course management and not using just plain common sense. It, however, makes for a great movie.

Whatever the reason that Tiger's shot went astray, you can see how it could easily, and probably did, fit into one of the mental aspects. What makes Tiger so great, is that it happens so seldom.

[9]Tour Tempo.com

NOTES

~~~~~~~~~~~~~~~~~~~~

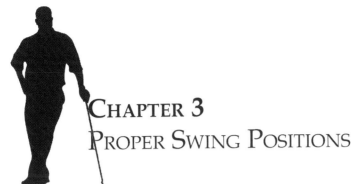

CHAPTER 3
PROPER SWING POSITIONS

As mentioned in the first chapter, great players have three physical things in common. First, and most importantly, is the impact position. The left side (right side if a lefty) always arrives at the ball first, and the club head does not pass the hands at impact with the ball. Secondly, they maintain the triangle from address through the impact zone. Third, they maintain their balance, which is evident in their finish.

The impact position is by far the biggest fault I see in amateurs. The club head is flipped at the ball, rather than swung through it. This is caused from trying to hit the ball instead of just swinging. At impact, there is a momentary stopping to hit the ball, which slows the club head down, puts loft on the club, and the shaft loses its torque. It is very much like trying to push a rope.

Picture for a moment the paddle ball we have all played with. You know, the one that has a ball attached to a long rubber band that is attached to a wooden paddle? Well, take the rubber band off the paddle, and by holding the tip of the rubber band, begin to swing the rubber band around in a circle out in front of you, but just over your head, trying to see how fast you can make the ball go. Pretty darn fast!

Now try to make it go faster by moving your hand toward the ball, thereby taking the tension out of the rubber band, while still swinging it over your head. Doesn't go as fast does it?

This is the effect that occurs when you try to hit the ball and let the club head pass your hands. It is an awful position, and can cause any number of bad weak shots to the right, or even pull hooks.

If you have ever seen stop action photos of these great players, you

you can clearly see that basically a triangle that was formed at address is kept, and the lines remain straight. Since we remember in pictures, the pictures on the next pages of my swing illustrate the proper golf swing positions, the correct and incorrect impact position, as well as the address triangle position, the triangle at impact, and the balanced finish.

Now again, I don't pretend to be in the category of the great golfers we have talked about, but if you will study these pictures, you will begin to understand how throwing the club head completely breaks down the golf swing at impact. If this occurs, you can see from the different club angle of attack, that anything is possible, but rarely does it result in a good golf shot.

Okay, the million dollar question. How do we get ourselves in the correct impact position? First you must start with the proper address.

Triangle at Address Position

As you can see from the photo, the address is relaxed, feet are about shoulder width apart, arms hang down naturally, weight is evenly distributed, the ball position, for this five iron, is three inches or so inside the left heel, the head is behind the ball, and there is a relatively straight line from the left shoulder to the club head, but is not forced forward into a perfectly straight line.

The following illustrations depict the correct and incorrect postures. As can been seen in the drawing, and the illustration that follows it, the ideal position is to have the arms hang down naturally, with them just outside the toe line. From this position you are able to appropriately adjust the distance that you need to stand for each club, furthest away with the driver, and moving closest with the wedges.

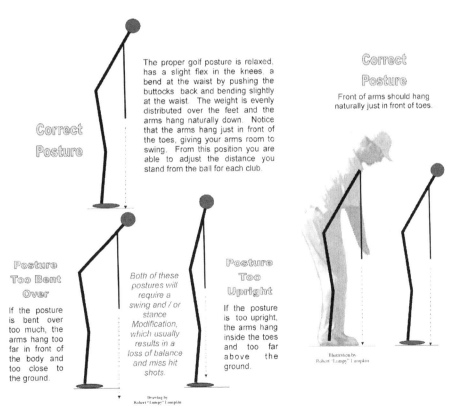

Correct Posture

The proper golf posture is relaxed, has a slight flex in the knees, a bend at the waist by pushing the buttocks back and bending slightly at the waist. The weight is evenly distributed over the feet and the arms hang naturally down. Notice that the arms hang just in front of the toes, giving your arms room to swing. From this position you are able to adjust the distance you stand from the ball for each club.

Correct Posture

Front of arms should hang naturally just in front of toes.

Posture Too Bent Over

If the posture is bent over too much, the arms hang too far in front of the body and too close to the ground.

Both of these postures will require a swing and / or stance Modification, which usually results in a loss of balance and miss hit shots.

Posture Too Upright

If the posture is too upright, the arms hang inside the toes and too far above the ground.

Illustration by
Robert "Lumpy" Lumpkin

Drawing by
Robert "Lumpy" Lumpkin

The backswing begins by pushing the club away with the back of the left shoulder, not lifting the club with the hands. Notice that the toe of the club points to the sky in a square position. The weight has begun moving to the inside of the right foot, and the shoulders and hips are beginning to turn around the body, while the head remains steady.

One of the worst pieces of advice I have ever heard is to 'keep your head down'. The correct advice is to keep your posture. Trying to keep your head down can create a turtle shell and not allow the shoulders, hips and arms to properly rotate around the body. All golfers' heads move a little bit, but the idea is to keep it steady by maintaining the correct posture.

At the top of the backswing the weight has moved to the inside of the right foot, the shoulders have rotated 90 degrees, and the hips have rotated 45 degrees. This has created the 'back to the target position'. The head is behind the ball, the wrists are fully cocked, and the toe of the club is basically pointed to the ground in a square position.

Notice the left arm is straight, but not locked or rigid. Every swing is unique, and you will notice that because of a previous back injury, my swing has a slight tilt to it. So, no matter what your unique characteristics might be, you can still get the club back to the proper impact position.

As you begin your downswing, the sensation you will have is as though you are pulling the butt end of the club down to your right foot. When you begin your downswing, *you must not start by throwing the club from the top*.

Throwing the club from the top is commonly called casting, as in fishing. This is a terrible move and can cause an over the top and an outside in swing.

Instead, the club is pulled down with the left hand, as you begin to uncoil your hip and shoulder turn, and begin a subtle shift of your weight to the left side.

Again, on the downswing, the sensation you will have is as though you are pulling the butt end of the club down to your right foot. Notice that the toe of the club is again pointed to the sky. As you approach the impact zone, you should feel as though the left side is approaching the ball like a back hand in tennis, with the right side following. In the modern swing, the leg drive is not as important as it was in the old reverse "C" swing. It is more of a pulling with the left side, and a rotating around the body, instead of an up and tilt, as you can see by the arrows in the following extension photo.

As is evident in the incorrect impact position, the triangle is broken down, the club head has been flipped, and the hands are still at impact. By the hands remaining at impact, it shows what we have discussed earlier about the momentary stopping to hit the ball has occurred.

Incorrect Impact Position   Correct Impact Position

The space between the legs is less in the correct position, indicating that there was no interference in releasing the club. Also, notice that when the ball is struck, the left side is straight and firm. This increases both the power and accuracy of the shot. Study these two pictures carefully, and really understand the difference between hitting at the ball, and swinging through the ball.

As you go through impact, the feeling is like the back of the left hand is slowly beginning to roll to the ground. This is what squares the club head at impact and closes the face, as it passes through the impact zone. How much the face closes determines the flight of the ball: either straight, draws or fades. Notice that the toe of the club is pointing to the sky.

Here's a little drill for you to try. We have all probably swung a baseball bat at some time in our lives. Go ahead and make a baseball swing at chest height with your golf club. You will notice that you naturally move your weight to the right side on the backswing and to your left side on the forward swing. You will also notice how your hands and arms naturally role over as they pass right in front of you. With some obvious adjustments, this is the golf swing, but on a different plane. I know that may sound strange at first, but I can assure you that it is extremely close to the same.

In the extension through the ball, you can see the weight has moved to the left side with the right heel coming up off the ground.

The Old
Reverse
"C" Swing

Also illustrated in the picture, by the arrows, is the arc that the body bends into in the old reverse "c" position. You can see why the back takes a great deal of stress in this type of swing. This is one of the things that prompted the move toward the modern type swing.

You can clearly see the back of the right hand, which means the left hand has rolled under, squaring and closing the club face. Also notice that the triangle is still intact, and there is no "chicken wing", which is caused when the left arm breaks down, giving way to hitting the ball with the right hand.

It must be further understood that when you momentarily stop to hit the ball, and you hit it with the right side, your turn also stops in order to keep your right hand on the club.

Try this yourself and make a swing to the impact position, and throw your right hand at the ball. Now, without turning your body, extend your left arm straight toward your target and try to keep the right hand on the club. It is not possible.

I have to relate this explanation by J. C. Anderson from a video clip on the secrets of what the pros know about the golf swing.

Quote: "I try to flat load my feet, so I can snap load my power pack, that way I can magnify both the lag and drag pressure through impact fix, as long as my number two power accumulator doesn't break down, I can reach maximum centrifugal force with minimum pivotal resistance. You see the pivot is the use of multiple centers to produce a circular motion for generating centrifugal force on an adjusted plane plus maintains the necessary balance to deliver up to a two line delivery path. See golf is geometrically oriented for a linear of force. It involves a physical muscular thrust and the geometry of the circle. You can divide the golf swing into twenty four basic components each having twelve and fifteen different variations. Now when you think of all this and you get it all set, hopefully you'll hit shots like this..." end quote, as he tops the ball, catches it, throws it down the fairway and then poses in a balanced follow through.

If you have never seen this clip, he not only relates the entire lines without missing a beat, but he also does it as a speed talker. Hope this will help you see the opposite end of the spectrum: the natural golf swing inside you.

The result of a natural swing, without hitting at the golf ball, is a well balanced finish. About 90 percent of the weight has now transferred to the left side. From this balanced position you are able to lift your right foot. You have probably read and/or heard about the belt buckle facing the target on your finish. The right heel is now off the ground, with the right knee also facing the target.

NOTES

~~~~~~~~~~~~~~~~~~~~

CHAPTER 4
THE INSIDE PATH

All right, what have we learned up to this point? Mentally, great golfers trust their golf swings, accept their environment as all part of the game of golf, and swing their natural swings within themselves creating timing, rhythm and tempo.

Physically they have three things in common. First, and most importantly, is the impact position. The left side (right side if a lefty) always arrives at the ball first and the club head does not pass the hands at impact with the ball. Second, they maintain the triangle from address through the impact zone. Third, they maintain their balance, which is evident in their finish, and is the direct result of their timing, rhythm and tempo.

You have learned how to develop these same attributes. Of course, how well you perfect and maintain the attributes depends on the time spent on each. But let me give you some encouragement. It takes doing something approximately fifteen minutes a day, for thirty consecutive days, for it to become a habit.

When Mr. Furgason first began teaching me, he said my golf swing looked like a drunken monkey falling out of a tree. Okay, got a picture of that? Listen, my golf swing was so bad that I sliced the ball forty degrees from left to right. Golfers on the course were requesting hard hats as I aimed right at them on the other fairway or tee box.

I recall one time that I had to aim at the cars in the parking lot just to be able to hit the fairway. To say I had a banana slice would be the understatement of the century! To steal a quote: "If I grew tomatoes, they would come up sliced!"

My assigned drill was to swing in my back yard until I created 'half moon shape' type semi-divots in the grass. In other words, mow the grass with my five-wood. It took me about thirty days or so. Remember, I have not hit a single golf ball in all this time.

I did, however, have a strange looking back yard!

So I met up with Mr. Furgason at the golf range. He walked out to the range with one golf ball. That's correct, just one golf ball. He said, "If you hit this ball down the fairway with a draw, I will continue to teach you. If you fail, find someone else's time to waste." Wow, talk about pressure. So I made a few warm up swings and then stepped up to the ball. I said to myself, he is either right, and that all the work I had put in is going to work, or it isn't.

To my great pleasure, the ball rocketed down the middle of the fairway with the most beautiful draw I had ever seen. Of course, for the ball to move from right to left, instead of a forty degree slice, was a miracle to me. True to his word, Mr. Furgason continued to teach me and even caddied for me in my first Monday tour qualifier.

The next picture illustrates an overhead view of the inside half moon swing path. The right picture is throwing the club outside in and the left picture is the approach for the correct inside impact position.

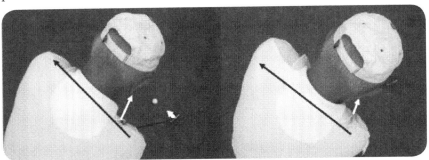

Notice the shoulder angle and the difference in the distance between the ear and the shoulders, for the inside approach to the ball on the left.

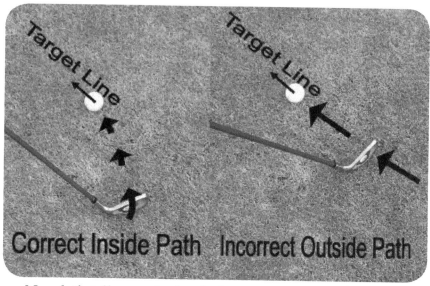

Now let's talk more in depth about the inside swing path. The sensation you will feel is usually that you are swinging flat and around your body. A great instructor, and now commentator, Peter Kostas wrote a book many years ago about the inside swing path. I was fortunate to have been given that book by Mr. Furgason. It reinforced the inside swing that Mr. Furgason was teaching me.

The great Jack Nicklaus endorsed very few products in his career. However, one that he did endorse is "The Inside Approach to Better Golf." This is an excellent training aid and I highly recommend that you get and practice with this remarkable training system. It comes complete with the "inside approach" DVD to assist you in understanding the inside golf swing.

The following diagrams illustrate the proper path that the golf club should be swung on and the path that it should not be swung on. Study these pictures and diagrams, and see the dramatic difference in the two paths.

The club is thrown over the top

In a lot of cases the feet are not open which restricts the rotation

Incorrect swing path

The club is swung from the top and usually steep. The result is an outside to in golf swing usually creating a slice because the club face is left open. If the clubface is closed it creates a pull hook.

Drawing by Robert "Lumpy" Lumpkin

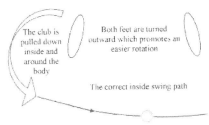

The club is pulled down inside and around the body

Both feet are turned outward which promotes an easier rotation

The correct inside swing path

The club is swung from the inside and then back around the body after impact. In other words, if playing baseball you are swinging inside toward right field.

What is important to learn here is that I know from first hand experience that repeating something for thirty days does work. In addition to this, I have had the distinct honor to witness many of my students have such a revelation. With their permission, some of my student's quotes are published in this book. My students' ages have ranged from 5 to 87.

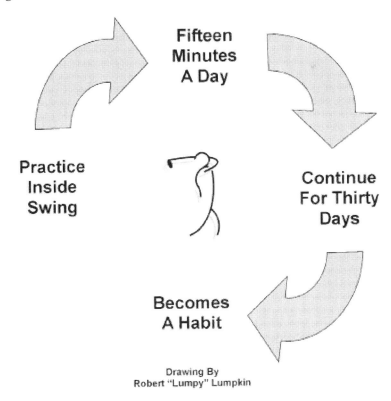

Fifteen Minutes A Day

Practice Inside Swing

Continue For Thirty Days

Becomes A Habit

Drawing By
Robert "Lumpy" Lumpkin

NOTES

~~~~~~~~~~~~~~~~~~~~~

CHAPTER 5
SWING FAULTS
THE SMASH FACTOR

Most amateur golfers have one or more of the deadly swing faults. These faults can cause a myriad of golf shots. The swing faults are: swinging too upright on the backswing, keeping their feet pointed straight, throwing the club from the top, a reverse weight transfer, failing to roll the hands at impact, swinging outside to in, flipping the club at impact, and not releasing the club.

Let's take the swing faults one at a time. Swinging the club too upright on the backswing is usually caused from either a misunderstanding of the proper path, or the lack of a shoulder turn from the waist.

The shoulder turn is 90 degrees while the hip turn is 45 degrees. A lot of golfers only turn their shoulders about 45 degrees, which causes them to lift the club upwards, or too steep, in order to complete their backswing.

Think about it this way. You want to turn the club back with your left shoulder and allow the hands to go over the right shoulder. For those that have been swinging too steep, you will think you are swinging flat. Flat, however, is usually caused from laying the club off at the top as opposed to the hands being below the right shoulder.

Entertainer & Musician Richard Hubbell. Richard is sixty something, but notice the 90 degree shoulder turn and 45 degree hip turn. Notice also the toes are pointed out 20 to 30 degrees. Richard is about a four handicap. Well done Richard!

This picture of an amateur golfer demonstrates the proper shoulder turn, hip turn, and feet placement. Notice that the left arm is bent. While a straighter arm is preferred, you never want the left arm to be rigid or locked. This little flex in his arm does not hurt his golf swing.

Keeping the feet pointed straight restricts the shoulder turn. Open both toes 20 to 30 degrees to the line of flight. This will allow you to make the 90 degree shoulder turn, and the hips will follow.

Richard is a great friend of mine and I have had the pleasure of playing golf with him many times. A few years back, during a practice round for a tournament he was preparing for, he was struggling with his swing. He asked me if I saw anything, and I had noticed that he was not rotating his left hip around through the swing. I grabbed his left pocket and pulled it around so he could feel the correct movement.

Well, he proceeded to give me a thumping on the course that day. He blasted his next drive well over 300 yards and continued to hit it past me the rest of the round. He went to a Senior U. S. Open qualifier and shot 76, missing the tournament qualifying by six shots. For those of you that like to play tournament golf, be sure to pay attention to the advice in chapter fourteen, 'Playing Competitive Golf'.

As we have discussed, throwing the club from the top is commonly referred to as casting. What really happens is that the golf club is started in the downswing with the right side throwing, rather than the left side pulling. There are several reasons that a golfer does this, but most commonly, it is because he is in a hitting mode instead of a swinging mode.

For example, if you have ever experienced horseplay in a locker room with the flipping of the towels, you know that you do not throw the towel, but rather whip it. Tug-of-war is another good example. No one has ever won a tug-of-war by trying to push the rope. So think about having a rope or towel in your hands at the top of the golf swing. Actually take a large bath towel and give it a try. You will quickly learn the difference in throwing the club and swinging the club.

Weight transfer in a golf swing is often misunderstood. It is simply allowing 70-80% of your weight to move to the inside of the back foot on the backswing, and then allowing the same weight to transfer to the outside of the front foot on the forward swing.

A reverse weight transfer is when the golfer puts his weight on the left side on the backswing, and on the right side in the downswing. This reverse weight transfer usually causes over the top golf swings, again creating an outside-to-in swing. It also causes the club to be swung upwards instead of down in the downswing. If you have this fault, you probably have difficulty hitting the ball off tight lies, and prefer longer fairway grass. To correct this fault, practice making baseball type swings at chest level with your golf club. Make sure you "rare back" on your right side in the backswing and move to your left side on the forward swing.

George, a great friend of mine for more than thirty-five years, is a good example of this. He was a golf professional around college age and went on to have an outstanding career as a lawyer, and now a sitting judge. He has always had a reverse weight transfer and has struggled to correct it his entire golfing life, and acknowledges that it has prevented him from playing better golf. Keep working on it George; it's getting better.

Failing to roll the hands at impact can cause a slice or fade, even if you have the correct swing path. Leaving the club face open is the result, and it also adds loft to the club. After the ball is struck, it is going to turn to the right. If the path was correct, the ball starts to the right and turns to the right. If the path was outside, then the ball starts to the left, and slices back to the right.

To properly understand the rolling of the hands, visualize the back of the left hand rolling down to the ground as you swing through the ball. The baseball swing is also a great drill because almost all golfers naturally roll their hands when swinging at chest level.

This is absolutely certain…If you do not learn to roll your hands properly, you will never hit a draw.

Before Rolling Of Hands   **Correct Rolling**   **Incorrect Rolling**

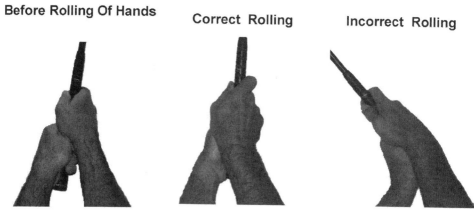

Photos by JEB

While we are on the rolling of the hands, it is important to point out that creating a draw swing will give you more distance, especially with the 'Big Dog'. It is worthwhile spending extra time learning how to draw the ball. Not only does the right to left ball flight go through the wind better, it runs when it hits the ground.

Swinging outside-to-in is illustrated in the previous pictures, as well as the correct inside path. The outside-in path is created by any one of the previous faults we have discussed, as well as flipping the club at impact. We have already discussed the way to swing the club inside, so let's move on to flipping the club at impact and the releasing of the club.

Right as the club is about to make contact with the ball, you must resist the natural tendency of hitting the ball, and release the club instead. This topic is not well written about, because it is misunderstood by amateur golfers and instructors alike.

Bottom line, the club is released when it is allowed to follow the path it's being swung on. Realize that the club can be moving more than 100 miles per hour at impact. Understand also, that the entire golf swing only takes about two seconds! The moment of impact is only two tenths of those two seconds.

Do you really think, in two tenths of a second, that we can consciously control that release of speed that we have generated? Of course not, but we can interfere with its natural path and timing by trying to control it. So here we go again, don't try to hit the ball, *just let the ball get in the way!*

Okay, we have learned all the necessary techniques, drills and (physical fitness in a later chapter), to hit the ball further. Putting all these together will create what has been referred to as the "smash factor". Here is my version of the smash factor.

The *smash factor* is the combination of club head speed, angle of attack, and the ball being struck directly on the sweet spot of the club. In other words, the swing has created the perfect angle that the club head strikes the ball, which is somewhere between one degree down angle to one degree up angle, with the ball perfectly struck in the center of the club face from an inside swing path, with the hands rolling, while no interference is experienced during the release of the club head, with the club head traveling at the greatest speed the golfer is able to create.

Wow, bet you didn't know that you had just learned all that! Simply put, the ball must be struck from the inside, on the sweet spot, in order to gain the most distance. It is true that a slower swing speed, striking the ball on the sweet spot of the club face, will make the ball travel further than a ball struck on the heel or toe with a faster club head speed.

So, once again, it comes back to your own natural swing inside you. Your ultimate success will depend upon how well you use your own natural timing, rhythm and tempo, along with how fast you can swing on the correct inside path, while still maintaining your balance, and how well you apply all that you have learned in the previous chapters.

Having been a participant in the National Long Drive competition, I have seen some of the biggest hitters in golf. I have also had the pleasure of playing golf with John Daly and Davis Love III in their prime, who as you know can whack the cover off. I worked for two years on doing nothing but hitting the ball further, and have an official drive of 406 yards. Yeah, I know my friends tease me, but there was only a 10 mile per hour tailwind, not 50 miles per hour like they claim.

That, of course, was also in my prime. Now closing in on 60 years of age, I still move the ball out there over 300 yards on occasion, with my average drive being about 275 yards. So for all you seniors, here's a great tip. Get a heavy-driver-training-aid, and go to work!

From 1993 Fantasy Golf Camp Brochure
Left to right: Robert Colbert, Jack Haley, John Daly, Greg Rita, Mike Standly, Robert "Lumpy" Lumpkin

NOTES

~~~~~~~~~~~~~~~~~~~

CHAPTER 6
STUDENTS' QUESTIONS, GRIP, AND PUTTING

Through the years, I have been asked many questions from my academy students, as well as call in questions from the radio audience, when I was the Official Golf Instructor for the 'Grand Strand Golf Channel Amateur Tour'. I thought it would be good to share some of those with you as we move into how to play the game of golf, course management, proper etiquette and specialty shots.

Radio Question – Is it true that the shaft is the engine of the swing? Yes. While there are a lot of components that go into how well you can swing a club, the flex of the shaft is at the top of the list, along with the swing weight. If the shaft is too stiff, then too little kick occurs in the swing; and if too soft, too much kick occurs. If the swing weight is too heavy, the club cannot be delivered with the maximum velocity; and if too light, a loss of distance will most likely occur.

This brings us to the last of the components that allow us to not only hit the ball further, but also to play the game at our best. Being a certified professional club builder and club fitter, I have seen many players improve beyond their wildest dreams by simply having the right equipment. Manufacturers today make such a variety of clubs, shafts and grips, that virtually anyone can improve their game with a properly fitted set of clubs. If you have not been properly fitted, you need to put that on the top of your golfing list.

Did you know that with a standard set of 14 golf clubs, excluding the putter, there are 13 different swing planes? What determines the plane is the lie angle and the length of the club. Trying to swing the driver on the same plane as the pitching wedge can cause an upright swing plane, as well as result in high weak slices or over-the-top pulls. I know, you have probably been told that there is only one swing plane. Try it yourself, and hold both a driver and a wedge with both the club heads behind the ball. Then stand where you would for the wedge and look at how upright it is compared to where you would stand for the driver.

Of course, just recently it is being promoted that you either have a one plane or a two plane swing. This, however, refers to whether your downswing plane mirrors your backswing plane, or does your downswing plane change. Perhaps the best example of this would be that Jim Furyk has a two swing plane, and Steve Stricker has a one swing plane. But again, this refers to whether the backswing and downswing plane mirror each other, or are different.

Radio Question—I keep hitting the ball fat. What are the main causes? Can you help me? Assuming that you are keeping your posture throughout the swing, there are only two main causes. If you decelerate at impact, or you throw the right hand at impact, you are likely to strike the ground before the ball. Deceleration usually occurs because a player has taken too big of a backswing for the shot at hand. Throwing the right hand usually occurs because a player tries to hit the ball too hard.

Always select the right club for the distance. Too much club can cause you to decelerate, while too little club can cause you to swing too hard.

Radio Question—What is the easiest way to draw or fade a golf ball? To draw the ball, aim a few yards right of your target and close the club face a few degrees, and then make your normal swing. To fade the ball, do just the opposite. Be sure to take one less club when playing the draw, and one more club when fading the ball. Practice how much you draw or fade the ball, because each player is different.

In Jack Nicklaus's book, "Golf My Way", he explains that he used this method repeatedly during his career. It is also the way Mr. Furgason taught me to draw and fade the ball. It is so much easier than trying to judge, right at impact, how much to roll or hang on, in order to hit the draw or fade.

Some golfers believe that changing the grip to a weaker or stronger position will help draw or fade the ball. While there is some truth to this, the grip is the most fickle part of the swing. Once you have a comfortable grip and it works, stick with it. The picture that follows illustrates the old and modern grip.

There are basically three types of grips. The ten finger grip, which is the photo on the right, the interlock which is the picture on the left, and the overlap grip, that looks similar to the left photo. Whichever grip you choose, the "V's" that form between the thumb and hand should both point somewhere between the chin and the right shoulder. The grip in the photo on the right is incorrect.

The following pictures illustrate the placement of the golf club in both the right and left hands. The most expedient way I have found to explain how to relate the gripping of the golf club is to 'shake hands with the grip'. The grip is placed across the left hand at a diagonal. It is not placed in the fingers or the palm, but rather as a combination of both.

As you can see in the photo, the club is behind the meat of the left hand and not in the palm or the fingers. If the grip is held too much in either the palm or the fingers, it affects the wrist cock and the club release.

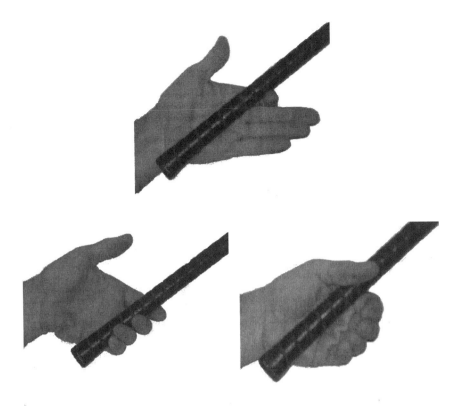

The top photo is the correct placement; the left photo is too much in the fingers, and the right photo too much in the palm

The club is gripped with the last three fingers of the left hand. The index finger wraps around the club and touches the thumb, creating a sort of pinchers. However, the index finger and thumb do not grip the club, but rest comfortably on the club to lend support.

The right hand grip is also held behind the meat of the hand. The two middle fingers of the right hand are all that grips the club. The index finger is either placed over the little finger of the left hand for an overlap grip, or is placed between the little finger and the ring finger for an interlocking grip.

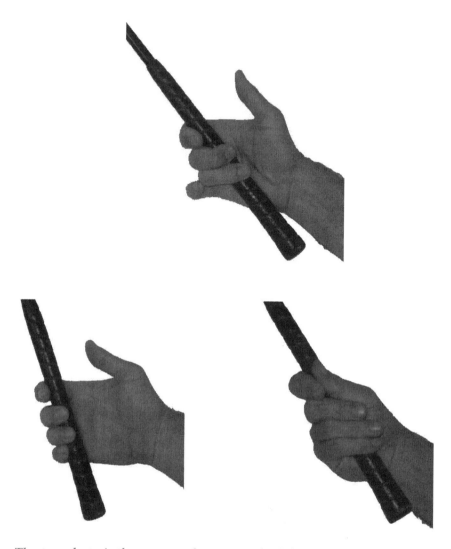

The top photo is the correct placement; the left photo is too much in the fingers, and the right photo too much in the palm

The grip pressure that is utilized is no more than necessary to hang onto the club, and not throw the club when you swing. If you were holding a baby bird, you would not exert enough pressure to harm the little fella.

The completed overlap grip is shown in the next group photo.

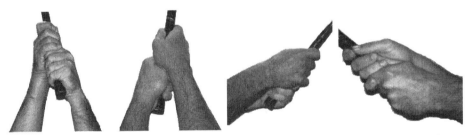

One final question and we will move on. Everyone wants to be a better putter. Several students have asked me: <u>What is the most important thing in putting, and how can I improve?</u> <u>Are there any practice drills that can help?</u>

Putting, first and foremost, should be fun. Concentrating too hard and trying to mechanically make putts leads to real problems. Some great advice is something I heard on one of Dr. Bob Rotella's[5] training tapes. He related: just look and react, very much like a heavily guarded basketball player does. A basketball player can be wide open and throw an air ball, but have three players jumping in his face, and whoosh, nothing but net.

Dr. Rotella also said that sometimes a player might be better off, if they did not putt in just a couple of seconds after addressing the ball; that another player could steal his ball, and then would have to add strokes to his score for slow putting. I don't believe he means to carelessly hurry, but too much time is spent standing over putts. Dr. Bob Rotella's books and tapes are available online and in book stores, and I highly recommend that you check out his materials.

Another great set of tapes to get are those from Dr. Lewis Smith[7]. His series of tapes include a combination of self-hypnosis, positive persuasion, and subliminal messages. In order for the self-hypnosis to happen naturally, all you have to do is relax in a quiet place where there will be no interruptions.

Dr. Smith's four subliminal messages are: "relax, feel good through the ball", "make your perfect swing", "play your best", and "enjoy yourself." If you listen to his tapes for fifteen minutes a day for thirty days, he guarantees you will see results.

Putting is designed to be fifty percent of your score in golf. That's Right! Meaning, on a par 72 course, if you hit all the greens in regulation, you have (36) putts to make par. Since a golfer rarely hits all greens in regulation, we should strive to have just 28-32 putts per round. The easiest way to make more putts is to focus on the speed and line. *Speed is, without a doubt, the most important thing in putting.*

Having fun is one of the best ways to relieve tension. Several years ago, I had the pleasure of playing a par three hole with the great Fuzzy Zoeller. Yes, he is as relaxed and has as much fun on the course as he appears to have on TV.

Watching his approach to putting was not only great fun, but he appears to just look and react. Fuzzy, if you read this book, I hope I got it right.

1998 @ Wild Wing Plantation, Myrtle Beach, SC
Left to right: Fuzzy Zoeller, Dave Rago, Robert "Lumpy" Lumpkin

A good drill is to put tees at three, ten, fifteen and twenty feet. Focus only on the line and the speed required. You will be surprised at how many times you can hit something as small as a tee, thus making the hole seem very large. We will discuss more about putting in the chapter on practice.

NOTES

~~~~~~~~~~~~~~~~~~~~

CHAPTER 7
SPECIALTY SHOTS

Specialty shots, when practiced, can lower your score. We have already talked about how to draw and fade the ball. Next we will cover uphill, downhill and side hill lies. Here is the general rule of thumb: The ball will travel in the direction of the slope; always play the ball toward the high foot; and take less club on a downhill lie, and more club on an uphill lie.

When you line up your shot, remember that an uphill lie generally goes to the left, so aim a little to the right. This occurs because the face of the club will come through to the left on an uphill lie. Also, the ball is going to come out high on the uphill lie, so use one more club. Always play the ball toward the high foot on the hill, and tilt the upper body with the slope of the hill.

On the downhill lie, the ball generally goes to the right, so aim a little to the left. This occurs because the face of the club will come through to the right on a downhill lie. The ball will usually come out quite low, so take one less club. Again, always play the ball toward the high foot on the hill, and tilt the upper body with the slope of the hill.

Photo by Robert "Lumpy" Lumpkin

Uphill lie, play ball towards the high foot, tilt with the hill, take one more club, aim a little right[1]

Downhill lie, play the ball towards the high foot, tilt with the hill,
take one less club, aim a little to the left [1]

The adjustment for the hilly lies, making sure you tilt the upper
body with the slope of the hill, is very important. This, however, can
be hard to conquer. During one of my golf clinics, one of the ladies
had a difficult time with it, and called herself 'tilt challenged'. She
did, however, eventually get the technique, and it has helped her on
her home course, because those type lies come along frequently. She
now no longer is so concerned about hitting the ball onto the moguls.

When the ball is above your feet, you will need to choke down on the club, and since the ball generally travels in the direction of the slope, you need to aim a little to the right. Play the ball a little back of center, and keep your balance by swinging smooth and taking one more club.

Side Hill Lie, Ball Above Feet, Aim to the Right, Choke Up on the Club

When the ball is below your feet, you will need to squat down to the ball, because we cannot lengthen our club. Since the ball generally travels in the direction of the hill, you need to aim left when the ball is below your feet. Play the ball in the middle of the stance, or slightly back. The tendency is to lean back to keep your balance, so if you have the ball too far forward in your stance, you can easily pull the ball to the left, rather than the ball going to the right. For all of these types of lies, make sure you swing well within yourself in order to maintain your balance and make solid content.

Photo By Robert "Lumpy" Lumpkin

Side Hill Lie, Ball Below Feet, Aim Left, Squat At Knees

Hard pan shots are difficult for most amateurs because it requires that the ball be struck first. This is a shot that flipping the club head, will cause you to hit behind the ball and bounce into it, or will cause you to hit it thin at the equator. And while we are covering this technique, it is the same technique you want to employ from a fairway bunker shot. Following is the secret you use on these shots.

Choke up on the club an inch or so. Play the ball toward your back foot. Take an extra club or two, keep your lower body steady, and swing mostly with just your arms. This shot is not about creating power, but making solid contact with the ball by ensuring that you strike the ball first.

DO NOT TRY TO LIFT the ball from this lie. Instead, make an extra effort to swing down smooth and steady. The extra club will take care of the distance for you. It is vitally important not to throw the club head at the ball; this can cause an injury and a terrible shot.

When in a fairway bunker, the first rule is getting out. If the lip poses a problem, take enough of a lofted club that you are sure you will clear the lip. If you watched the 2009 President's Cup, you saw a great player on the first hole hit the lip twice. All players make the mistake, from time to time; in thinking about the distance to the green, instead of rule one: When in trouble, get out safely!

In my golf schools, I demonstrate this shot and teach the students how to hit the shot consistently. Once you practice this technique a few times, it is relatively easy to become comfortable in any hard pan or fairway bunker situation.

I show my students how to hit the ball off roots, hard packed-down bare soil, wood that you might experience on a bridge, and even off the paved or concrete cart path, all using this technique.

We need to elaborate a little bit about playing a ball off a root. Be very careful that there is not a root interfering with the swing in front of or behind the ball. If this is the case, an adjustment to your swing is required, and in some cases the shot should not be played.

The most difficult root situation is when the ball is resting on one root, and there is a root in front and behind the ball. This takes practice, but an extremely upright backswing, with a very steep downswing is required, with an abbreviated follow through, stopping immediately after the ball is struck. Because an injury is very possible, several golf leagues allow a player relief as a local rule. This, of course, is not the case on tour or under the USGA rules.

A ball coming to rest on pine straw is a lie that is often found in the southern states. This shot is not a difficult shot to master fairly well. It is the same technique as the hard pan, with only one exception. Make sure you choke up the amount that the ball is perched above the ground, making your new swing path the correct height. The rest of the technique is the same.

On specialty shots, it is very important to keep the body still and quiet. None of the specialty shots require power, but instead, solid contact.

We have talked about fairway bunkers, but what about the greenside bunkers. This technique is totally different. The following drawing illustrates the correct stance for most greenside bunker shots.

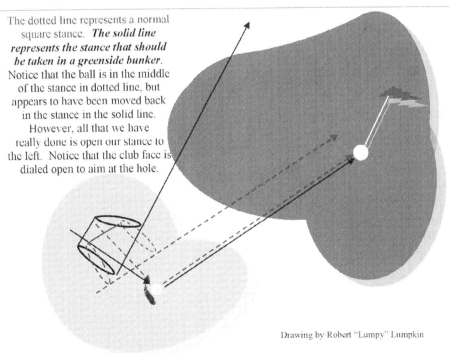

The dotted line represents a normal square stance. *The solid line represents the stance that should be taken in a greenside bunker.* Notice that the ball is in the middle of the stance in dotted line, but appears to have been moved back in the stance in the solid line. However, all that we have really done is open our stance to the left. Notice that the club face is dialed open to aim at the hole.

Drawing by Robert "Lumpy" Lumpkin

As you can see in the illustration, the club face is pointed where we want the ball to go. However, our stance is about forty-five degrees to the left. This promotes an out-to-in swing path, and the open face allows more loft. The secret to a good bunker shot is to make sure you hit the sand one to three inches behind the ball, and to keep the swing going through the shot.

So many amateurs try to either lift the ball out, or stab at the sand and just stop. This is probably the easiest shot in golf, because you do not have to strike the ball first. There is a three to four inch margin of error that will still result in a decent sand shot.

There are two basic types of sand, course and fine. The course sand is generally firmer and preferred by most pros because the distance and spin is easier to control. The course sand, when wet, can become quite packed, making it easier to hit a shot with less effort.

The fine sand is more difficult to play out of, because the club face can penetrate the softness very easily, making it more likely that you will dig into the sand too deep. The secret to playing out of fine sand is to make sure you allow the natural bounce of the sand wedge head to work, and to take a little flatter swing approach into the ball. In either case, make sure you twist your feet into the sand well enough to have a solid stance.

The hardest of the specialty shots is the dreaded 50 yard bunker shot. The reason this shot is more difficult is because the technique required employs a combination of the greenside bunker and fairway bunker techniques, plus an adjustment to your swing. To play this shot, move the ball back in your stance, choke up on the club about two inches, take a square to slightly open stance, and place about sixty percent of your weight on your left side. Make your normal swing plane going back with just your arms, while keeping your weight on the left side, and keeping your lower body very quiet. As you swing through the ball, you will have a feeling that you are leaning toward the target. This is normal and what you want. Make sure you make contact with the ball first, or no more than a half inch or so behind the ball. You will then want to make a follow through to about waist height or so. The swing should be very easy and smooth. It is not about power. Practice this shot, because it takes some getting use to.

Finally, we will address the left handed shot, (right handed for lefties). While this shot does not come into play real often, if you can understand how to hit the shot, it can be a shot saver. This shot is, of course, played with the club turned upside down. One thing that naturally happens when you do this is that the club will be aimed to your right. For this reason, you want to aim left, and also open your stance to avoid being hit by the ball. I do not recommend that you use a less lofted club than an eight iron.

Place the ball in the middle of your stance and put about sixty percent of your weight on the left side. This helps give the club a little loft. When you swing, do not take a full swing unless you can also play left handed. Take the club back about to shoulder height, and swing the club like you normally would, except not worrying about your follow through. Again, you need to practice this shot a lot on the range. Later in the book you will learn what happened to a pro, whose ball was just ten feet off the green, when he chose to play a left handed shot.

NOTES

~~~~~~~~~~~~~~~~~~~~~

Chapter 8
Properly Fitted Clubs

Certified professional club builders, and/or certified professional club fitters, are who you want to seek out for properly fitting your clubs. With today's technology in the manufacturing of club heads, grips, and shafts, I have yet to see a golfer, who with the proper clubs and fitting, did not improve their ability to play golf.

The reason for this is simple. First, let's talk about the shaft. The shaft must be the right weight and flexibility for you to get the most out of your golf swing. I have given this example to my students many times.

As a former track and field champion pole-vaulter, I know first hand that if the pole is too heavy, you cannot gain the proper speed running down the runway to plant the pole in the box. If the pole has too much flex, it will not properly lift you in the air to clear the bar. If the pole is too stiff, it will not assist you in getting airborne to gain the necessary height.

The shaft of your club works very much the same way. The flex helps you generate club head speed, as well as accuracy. Make sure you have your clubs shafts checked by a professional that is certified in club fitting.

The club heads in the irons, hybrids, fairway woods and driver need to look good to your eye. If you do not like the looks of a club, it will affect your ability to be positive about the club, and therefore the shot to be played. Next is the preference of player improvement clubs or tour blades. Not too many players use the blade any more, including the tour pros, because the other clubs are simply more forgiving on miss hit shots.

Should you use hybrid golf clubs? More and more pros are adding these clubs to their bags. What size driver head will work best for you? Should you have a heavy putter, and what length should it be? What is the best swing weight for your clubs?

Some of the other factors to consider in obtaining a properly fitted set of clubs are: Ball Velocity, Club Head Speed, Carry Distance, Power Transfer Ratio %, Launch Angle, Total Spin, Deviation, Angle of Descent, Angle of Attack, Side Spin, Club Face Angle, Trajectory, and Club Acceleration and Deceleration.

For proper club fitting go to a shop with certified personnel and the proper equipment

Any golfer who is serious about improving their game needs to be properly fitted at locations that have professionals who are certified in club fitting. The chances of buying a set of clubs that are right for you, without a proper fitting, is very slim. If you need someone to come to you for a fitting, I recommend Alvin Cloyd[19], if you live in the Myrtle Beach area. Al has a mobile tour trailer and is a master club builder.

Last year, a golfer from a northern state was on vacation and stopped in my shop. He was looking to gain more distance off the tee. He related that when he played with his regular golf group, all of them out drove him by twenty or thirty yards. He said he thought he was a better golfer than most of them, but could not figure out why he could not hit the ball as far as they were.

After a few test swings on our computerized simulator, it was apparent that he had a pretty good golf swing, but that his driver was not suited for him. I checked the shaft's frequency and it was an extra stiff shaft. After checking the swing weight, it was so heavy, it would be like trying to swing a ten pound sledge hammer.

After he settled on what driver head he most liked to look at, I built him a new driver with the correct shaft flex and swing weight. About two weeks later, he called and left me a message with such excitement and enthusiasm, he sounded like a kid in a candy store. He told me to tell everyone I know about his great improvement, and to use him as a reference. He was now hitting the ball forty to fifty yards further, and even hit one over three hundred yards. He made sure to tell me that he has a GPS yardage finder, and that what he was saying was absolute gospel. Now he can't wait each week to play in his regular group.

This type of reaction I have seen for years. Equipment in golf can truly improve your game. Can you imagine a football kicker trying to kick a fifty yard field goal with a defective and under inflated ball, or how about a baseball batter trying to get a hit swinging a bat that is made of wood so soft that the ball dents the wood. Without the proper equipment, it is very hard to excel in any sport, especially golf.

There is only one way to find out if your equipment is suited for you. Schedule an appointment with a certified professional and find out. You will be glad you did.

The grip is very important and should be changed frequently; how often depends upon how much golf you play. Basically, when the grip loses its tacky type feel, it's time to have them replaced.

<u>Now this is very important</u>. If you change the grip from the exact kind that you have on your clubs, make sure the technician keeps the swing weight of your clubs the same.

Grips weights can vary several grams, which can definitely change the swing weight significantly. If you have a forty gram weight grip and change to an eighty gram weight grip, your swing weight just got much lighter. It could go from D-2 to a light C swing weight, and, of course, the reverse is true. Insist that the grips are the same weight or that the club is counter balanced to keep the swing weight the same. The style and type of grip you choose, whether cord, semi-cord or non-cord, is an individual preference.

Remember, the grip is the only contact your body has with the club, so take time to decide which grip will work best for you. While on the topic of the grip, the Vardon or overlap grip has been attributed to the golfing extraordinaire, Harry Vardon.

For a moment, let's travel back in time and see how important it is to use the correctly fitted clubs, even without today's technology. The great Harry Vardon won British Opens way back in the late 1800's and early 1900's, and the U. S. Open in 1900. His book was originally published in 1905. The following is from his book, reprinted by Fredonia Books[20] in 2001.

"Let it only be said again that the golfer should do his utmost to avoid extremes in length or shortness. One hears of the virtues of fishing-rod drivers, and the next day that certain great players display tendency to shorten their clubs. There is nothin like the happy medium, which has proved its capability of getting the longest balls. The length of the club must, of course, vary according to the height of the player, for what would be a short driver for a six-foot man would almost be a fishing-rod to the diminutive person who stands but five feet high.

Let the weight be medium also; but for reasons already stated do not let it err on the side of lightness. The shaft of the club should be of moderate suppleness. As I have said, if it is too whippy it may be hard to control, but if it is too stiff it leaves too much hard work to be done by the muscles of the golfer."

19Alvin Cloyd, Al's Custom Golf Clubs, 843-602-5527
20Fredonia Books, Amsterdam, The Netherlands, www.fredoniabooks.com

NOTES

~~~~~~~~~~~~~~~~~~~~~

Chapter 9
Hit It Further / Golf Fitness

There has probably never been a golfer who hasn't wanted to learn to hit the ball further. Many of my students have learned how, and are amazed. As we look into this fascinating subject, I have provided some insights from other view points. Apply what you feel will help you in understanding how to hit the ball further.

Let The Big Dog Eat

While there is so much written about this subject, it all comes down to these simple issues. A golfer must develop proper flexibility, golf muscle strength, an inside golf swing path, proper impact position, and obtain properly fitted clubs (For Clubs see the previous Chapter 8).

In this chapter, you will learn how to stretch, gain more flexibility, build muscle strength, and how to hit it further.

Let's discuss what we mean by building our golf muscles. First of all, we do not mean be a body builder. How many great golfers fall into that category? That's correct; exactly none.

What we do want to do is exercise the golf muscles. There are a number of weighted training golf clubs that work great for this purpose. They come in all different kinds of clubs including the driver, iron and putter. Another great training tool is a heavy donut that slips over the shaft and slides down to the golf head.

Before swinging these weighted golf clubs, be sure to warm up and stretch just as if you were going to go play golf. To ensure that you maintain your timing, rhythm and tempo for your golf swing, always swing your regular club fifteen or twenty times when you finish with the heavy club. Also, it is a great idea to put the heavy club in the trunk and use it before you play to warm up and stretch your golf muscles. You can make several swings in the parking lot before you tee off.

A little caution is warranted here. Be careful when you first start with the heavy club not to injure yourself. It may surprise you just how tight your muscles really are.

A heavy driver will be one of the best investments you can make if you want to hit the ball further. The stronger and more flexible your hands, wrists and forearms are, the more club head speed you can generate. Yes, we need stronger legs because it is our foundation to a good swing just like the foundation of your house is vitally important; but the truth is that most of the club head speed is generated by the torso, shoulders, arms, hands and wrists. The torque of coiling and uncoiling the torso/stomach muscles generates a lot of speed. As you swing the heavy driver, you will begin to feel the muscles that are really working.

Again, for you to hit the ball further, you must develop proper flexibility, golf muscle strength, an inside golf swing path, proper impact position and obtain properly fitted clubs.

For those of you that enjoy the scientific approach, I recently came across this excellent explanation on the internet for you, and have reprinted it unedited on the next pages.

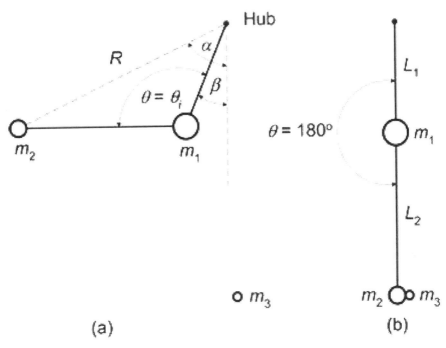

Physics Reveals the Key to a Great Golf Swing
December 18th, 2006

The simple double-pendulum model of the golf swing, showing key angles, lengths, and masses. For instance, m_1, m_2, and m_3 are the masses of the arms/hands, club head, and ball, respectively; L_1 is the length of the arms/hands, and L_2 is the length of the club head). (a) The system before the club is released and (b) when the club is about to strike the ball.

What happens when a golf-loving researcher injures a shoulder and can't play for three months? Rod White, a metrologist (measurement scientist), used the spare time off the course to undertake an analysis that revealed the foundation of an effective golf swing. As it turns out, it's all in the wrists.

"Even the most able golfers experience occasions when a ball hit deliberately with little effort inexplicably travels further than expected," said White, of technology company Industrial Research Ltd. in Lower Hutt, New Zealand, to *PhysOrg.com*. "But there is an explanation. A double pendulum model, which represents the golf swing reduced to its simplest elements, explains this effect and how to make a swing more efficient."

A double pendulum consists of one pendulum tacked on to the end of another. The upper pendulum swings from a fixed pivot point and the lower pendulum swings from the end of the upper one. In golf, the equivalent components are the shoulders (acting as the fixed pivot), arms and hands (the upper pendulum), and the club shaft and club head (the lower pendulum).

There are several factors influencing the efficiency of a golf swing. Among them are the length of the club, the length of the player's arms, the mass of the club head, the wrist-cock angle – how far backward the wrists are bent during the swing – and whether the wrists actively twist during the swing, resulting in wrist torque.

White's analysis is the first to consider wrist-cock angle. His model is also very simple in a Physics 101 kind of way, explaining the mechanics of the golf swing in terms of the club's changing moment of inertia. These two points distinguish his work from similar analyses by C.B. Daish[1] and the late University of Nebraska physicist Theodore

Jorgensen[2]. White shows that the energy and momentum of the arm-club system are redistributed during the swing as a direct result of the un-cocking of the wrists that takes place before the club strikes the ball.

"As the wrists un-cock near the bottom of the swing, the club head and the hands are moving in different directions, which means the club pulls against the hands and slows them down," White said. "This means, in turn, that the kinetic energy in the shoulders and arms is transferred to the club. Without wrist-cock, most of the kinetic energy stays in the arms and shoulders and the swing is inefficient. Best of all, the golfer does not have to do any extra work to make the transfer happen." Thus, wrist-cock is the make-or-break factor in a good golf swing.

The full range of motion of the double pendulum is described by two complicated equations. In fact, White says, they are too complicated to be of much help in a study of the golf swing. "They obscure the basic mechanism by which the golf swing derives its efficiency."

He simplified the equations by removing the components that account for radial motion – motion away from the shoulders, such as what would happen if the club handle slipped down slightly in the golfer's hands during the swing. There are two key points in the swing where radial motion does not factor in: at the end the first half of the swing when the golfer is holding the club at a fixed wrist-cock angle and about to release the club, and the instant before the club head strikes the ball, when the golfer's arms and the club line up vertically. By using these two snapshots, White broke the swing down into a much more basic and manageable system.

"This model helps explain why learning a good swing can be difficult," he concludes. "Both the extraordinary effectiveness of wrist cock in gaining distance (without having to do additional work) and the loss in distance that occurs with the application of wrist torque are counter-intuitive."

Citation: Rod White, "On the efficiency of the golf swing," *Am. J. Phys.*, **74** 1088-1094 (2006)

References:

[1] C.B. Daish, *The Physics of Ball Games.* (London: The English University Press, 1972)

[2] Theodore P. Jorgensen, *The Physics of Golf.* (Melville, NY: The American Institute of Physics, 1994)

By Laura Mgrdichian, Copyright 2006 PhysOrg.com

~~~~~End of Article~~~~~

Now for the rest of us, let me start with the muscle flexibility for all the golf swing positions, and injuries that could result from not being properly golf fit.

This excellent article, from Physiotherapy Clinic published on the internet, illustrates and explains the use of golf muscles, flexibility and exercises related to the golf swing. It is reprinted unedited.

During a golf swing the discs and ligaments of the spine are subjected to tremendous stresses, including: compression; rotation; shear and side bending. The average golfer takes about 9,000 swings per year, including rounds played and time spent practicing at the golf driving range. This high number of repetitions can potentially lead to an injury, even with a golfer who has sound mechanics, good strength and good flexibility.

The vast majority of golf injuries are not the result of single traumatic or freak accidents. Rather, they occur as a result of tissue damage sustained over time from overuse and poor technique.

How does the golf swing contribute to golf-related injuries?

Golf instructors and golf medicine experts divide the swing into phases. Each phase of the swing (the Address, Backswing, Downswing, Impact, and Follow-Through) places demands on certain parts of the body and can result in specific types of injuries. Injuries to body tissues during the golf swing are caused by excessive tissue tension, twisting, or the stress absorbed by the golfer due to impact of the club with the ball, or ground or rock or – whatever.

To properly prepare for the golf swing, you must first "address" the ball. The address is the least stressful golf swing phase. During the address phase, body weight is evenly distributed on both feet, which should be roughly shoulder-width apart. The spine is tilted forward from the hips so that the spine is positioned at a right angle (90 degrees) to the club shaft. The knees are then relaxed (flexed) to center the body weight over the feet. The arms are extended and relaxed. The address phase is not particularly stressful in itself, but mistakes in grip or stance can lead to injury-causing consequences later in the swing.

During the backswing, the club is raised to its highest point in the swing. Body weight is shifted to the right foot. Rotation of the hips, knees, shoulders, and spine occur, and the head remains relatively still. At the top of the backswing the left thumb, left wrist, and right wrist are in the cocked position, and the forearm muscles are stretched as far as they can be. Less than one in four golf injuries are thought to occur during the backswing phase.

During the downswing, the weight is shifted to the left foot while the knees, hips, and trunk rotate together to the left. A left-sided "uncoiling" occurs due to vigorous contraction of the abdominal muscles (the muscles responsible for rotating the trunk) and the spinal muscles. The abdominal muscles are working three times harder during the downswing phase than during the backswing. Similarly, the spinal muscles are working four to five times harder during the downswing, compared with the backswing. The right shoulder muscles (rotator cuff) and right pectoral muscles ("pecs") are also firing away. The pecs are now working six to seven times harder than they were during the backswing, in order to propel the club head (which accelerates to speeds of 100 miles per hour in about two-tenths of a second). Injuries during the downswing are about twice as frequent as backswing injuries.

At impact, the club makes contact with the ball - we trust and believe. The wrists and hands complete the acceleration of the club head, the wrists unhinging in a whip-like motion as the right hand rotates over the left after the ball is hit. Body weight shifts to the left. The force of impact from hitting the ball (called the counterforce) is transmitted up the club to the body. If an object other than the ball is struck by the club head (for example, the ground, a tree, a rock), the counterforce is greatly increased. Many muscles act together to keep the club head moving forward through the impact phase, effectively overcoming the counterforce. Without these hardworking muscles (which include the forearms, and shoulder rotator cuff muscles), the club would screech to a halt at impact. The majority of injuries related to the golf swing occur during the impact phase.

After striking the ball in the follow-through, the club gradually decelerates during the follow-through. The body rotates to the left around the spine. The wrists rotate about each other to create the "roll-over" motion of the hands. The hips and shoulders continue to rotate until the body is facing the target (or, in some cases, the body is facing the water hazard). The spine hyper extends, and body weight completely shifts to the left side. About one in four golf swing injuries occur during the follow-through phase. Lower back injuries are especially common.

Why stretch before golf? Stretching before you golf loosens your muscles and prepares them for what lies ahead. And there's more. Regular stretching can promote a fluid, full golf swing and help prevent injury. Before you stretch, warm up with five minutes of walking or another light activity. Then complete the series of golf stretches described below. Hold each stretch for 10 seconds. Repeat three to five times. Do one set of golf stretches every day and another set before and after each round of golf.

Start by stretching your quadriceps.

• Stand with your back to a chair or bench and cross your arms over your chest. Place your left foot on the chair or bench. Use a lower seated chair if it's more comfortable.
• Keep your left knee even with or behind your right knee. Tighten your left buttock muscles. You'll feel a stretch in the front of your left thigh.
• To mimic your follow-through, rotate your shoulders and torso to the right and bend your left shoulder and trunk slightly toward the ground.
• Repeat the stretch with your right foot on the chair.
Next stretch your back muscles.
• Stand with your feet apart facing the back of a chair.
• Grasp the back of the chair with your hands.
• Holding on to the chair and keeping your spine straight, move your body down and away from your hands until you feel a stretch near both armpits.

Now move on to your hamstring muscles.

• Hold your golf club behind your shoulders. Stand next to a step, low table or tee bench. Put your right foot on the step.

• Keep a slight bend in your right knee. Then bend your upper body forward at your hips, keeping your spine straight until you feel a comfortable stretch in the back of your right thigh.

• Maintain this stretch while rotating your shoulders and back to the left and to the right.

• Repeat with the left leg.

You can stretch your hips several ways. Try this stretch first:

• Sit on a chair, low table or tee bench. Place your right ankle on top of your left thigh.

• Push down on your right knee with your right forearm. Then lean forward at your waist until you feel a gentle stretch in your right hip.

• Repeat the stretch on the opposite side.

Then try this hip stretch:

• Sit on a chair, low table or tee bench. Raise your right knee up and grasp it with your left hand.

• Keeping your spine upright, pull your right knee up toward your left shoulder. You'll feel a stretch in your right buttock.

• Mimic the position of your right hip when you're at the top of your backswing by turning your shoulders to the right.

• Repeat the stretch on the opposite side.

Here's a final hip stretch:

• Kneel on your right knee, holding your golf club with your right hand. Place your left foot in front of you, bending your knee and placing your left hand on the leg for stability.

• Keep your back straight and abdominal muscles tight. Lean forward, shifting more body weight onto your front leg. You'll feel a stretch in the front of the hip and thigh of the leg you're kneeling on.

• Repeat the stretch on the left side.

Now stretch your wrists upward.

• Hold your right arm in front of you with your palm facing down.

• Keeping your elbow straight, gently pull your wrist up by grabbing the top of your fingers.

• Repeat three to five times on each wrist.

Stretch your wrists downward, too.

• Hold your right arm in front of you with your palm facing down.

• Keeping your elbow straight, gently pull your wrist down toward your body. You'll feel the stretch in your right forearm and wrist.

• Repeat three to five times on each wrist.

Next stretch your shoulders.

• Stand with your feet shoulder-width apart as though you're addressing the golf ball. Hold your left elbow with your right hand.

• Keeping your left thumb pointed up, bend your left wrist toward your left thumb.

• Rotate your trunk to the right.

• Pull on your left elbow until you feel a stretch in your back.

• When stretching the trailing (right) shoulder, grab your right elbow with your left hand. Then rotate your trunk to the left.

Finally, stretch your core muscles.

• Stand with your feet shoulder-width apart as though you're addressing the golf ball. Fold your arms across your chest.

• Initiate your backswing motion.

• Continue from the top of your backswing position to your follow-through.

• At home, you may want to try this stretch in front of a mirror to check the different positions of your swing.

Injuries

• The vast majority of golf injuries are not the result of single traumatic or freak accidents. Rather, they occur as a result of tissue damage sustained over time from overuse and poor technique. Most golf injuries fall into the general categories of strains, sprains, fractures, and tendonitis. The region of the body that is most susceptible to injury is the lumbar spine. This is because each full golf swing places the spine at (or near) the end-range of available spine movement. And this is true during the several phases of the golf swing, thus potentially setting up the golfer's lumbar joints, discs and muscles for micro-trauma.

• The elbow is the second most commonly injured area in golfers. The two most common problems are medial epicondylitis (also know as golfer's elbow) and lateral epicondylitis (more commonly known as tennis elbow). The golfer's elbow is thought to be caused by hitting the ground first, and tennis elbow may be caused by over-swinging with the right hand in the right-handed golfers. Both of these problems increase with age and frequency of play. Good pre-round stretching of the upper extremity and a good strengthening program has been shown to decrease these problems.

• Another commonly injured area in golfers is the shoulder. There are specific muscles in the shoulder that are most active in the swing. These are the subscapularis (one of the rotator cuff muscles), pectoralis ('Pecs') and latissimus ('Lats') muscles. Impingement syndrome (a bursitis and tendonitis in the shoulder), rotator cuff problems, and arthritis are the most common shoulder problems. A good warm-up routine and specific exercises that target the shoulder can help decrease the incidence of these injuries.

Physiotherapy Clinic
Room 409 Thaniya Building (BTS Wing)
4th floor, 62 Silom Road, Suriyawongse, Bangrak, Bangkok 10500
Phone: 662-632 8787, Fax: 662-632 8788

NOTES

CHAPTER **10**
PRACTICE

Practicing is an important part of excelling at anything you choose to do, especially sports. There are specific things you need to do to get the most out of practice. Knowing what, how, and the time to spend on each area is crucial to getting the most out of your practice time.

The saying, 'practice makes perfect', is really correct when rephrased to 'perfect practice makes perfect'. So it does no good to practice the incorrect swing techniques; all you accomplish is engraining bad habits. The longer you teach your muscles to remember how not to do it correctly, the longer it is going to take to make the changes that allow you to make the natural golf swing that is inside you.

We have all seen golfers out pounding golf balls. Hundreds of driver shots launched as far as can be hit. Golfers hitting bag after bag of range balls down range. While this is great exercise, and if you have never hit five hundred or more balls with a driver in one practice session, you have no idea what a workout it can be. It is, however, a futile effort in improving your game, unless it is for the purpose of competing in a long drive championship.

There was a time that I did just that. I spent hours upon hours of conditioning my body to withstand the riggers of going all out after a golf ball, because it was required for that purpose. If, however, you want to play great golf, I don't recommend spending more that twenty percent of your time with the driver. Why? ...Because it is the least used club in the bag. Think about it, if there are four par threes on the course and you use the driver off the tee on all the other holes, you

only make fourteen swings with the driver.

If the par for the course is seventy-two, here is the breakdown of the percent of usage of your fourteen entitled clubs. Assuming that you use thirty-two putts to complete your round, you will use an iron, hybrid or fairway wood twenty-six times, but the driver only fourteen, if you use it off all the par fours and fives.

Obvious what to spend most of your time practicing on, isn't it? Your practice time should be spent in this order; putting, chipping, specialty shots, irons, hybrids or woods, and the driver. With only having thirty-two putts, that is more than forty-four percent of your score of seventy-two, while your driver is only about nineteen percent.

Wow, you probably just never thought about it this way before. Now this <u>does not diminish</u> the importance of the driver, but you need to understand where the shots are most likely to be saved in order to shoot lower scores. The reason chipping is second is because it directly affects the number of putts. The closer you can get the ball to the hole, the fewer putts you are going to have.

Left to right: Richard Hubbell, John Robinson, Lumpy's Ball
Closest to Pin

Putting practice must be fun and simulate the putts you will have on the golf course. So here are some fun ways to practice. First, remember that the most important thing in putting is speed. If you miss the hole by one inch on either side of the hole, but hit the putt six feet past the hole, you still have to make a putt from six feet. If, however, you miss the hole by two feet left or right, but leave it hole high, you only have a two footer left.

To begin learning speed, just putt to a spot on the fringe and not the hole. You should select different distances of ten, fifteen, twenty and thirty feet. Choose both uphill and downhill putts. Putt until you can roll the ball to within inches of each of the distances.

Once you master this, go to the 'tee putting routine' that we talked about in chapter seven. Put tees at three, ten, fifteen and twenty feet. Start with three feet and work your way out. Putt six balls at a time and practice until you can hit the tee three or more times for each distance.

Then take one ball and putt to all the holes on the practice putting green. Practice until you can make fewer putts than an average of two per hole. So if there are six holes, you want to practice until you make less than a total of twelve putts. Remember, you are practicing to 'just look and react'.

If you have mechanical issues with your putting stroke, go see your professional golf instructor to help you out. However, we will briefly cover the basics of the putting stroke on the following pages.

The grip is an individual preference for each player. We have all seen the many different techniques in putting, including the grip. We have the claw, reverse, split handed, etc. The idea, however, is to take a grip that keeps the putter face square through the ball.

My personal favorite is a double overlap with the right little finger and right ring finger overlapping both the left index and left middle finger. Since I use the overlap grip for a full swing, it keeps everything very consistent. Jim Furyk uses this type of grip on his full swings as well.

These photos illustrate four different amateur golfers with numbers one and two using the "flipping action". Notice that number one has the club face open and number two has it closed. Number three has very little flip, but has left the face open. Number four, being the best example with very little flip, and the club face has remained square. Number four is more like what you are trying to achieve. At this time let me make sure that I am in no way making light of these golfers' effort. All of them pictured are friends of mine, unless now they want to shoot me for illustrating their techniques. Just joking of course; these are great guys I've played many pleasurable rounds with.

Basically, you want to create a pendulum type of putting stroke. You want to take the putter straight back and straight through. In reality, the putter swings slightly inside going back and slightly inside coming through. The reason for this is because if you keep your lower body quiet and still, and just rock your shoulders back and through, the club naturally swings on the inside path.

Some of the best putters in the world used to use a 'pop-type-stroke'. This is a putting stroke that is very wrist-y. I do not recommend this type of stroke because it is much more difficult to control.

When you address the ball, you want your eyes to be over the ball or just slightly inside the ball. The more over the line you are, the easier it is to see and stroke the ball on that line. You should also take a square stance to the intended line. Having said this, I personally prefer to use an open stance which allows my dominate eye to see down the line. To find your dominate eye, with both eyes open, hold your thumb up and cover an object in the distance. You will see two thumbs with one of the thumbs on the object. Close your left eye, and if the thumb stays on the object, you are right eye dominate.

This is important to know, not just in putting, but when lining up all shots. This is one reason that a lot of golfers line up their shots to the right of the target. They see the line with the non-dominate eye.

When I say to take a stance square to the intended line, I mean that your feet should be parallel to that line. The following illustration depicts what your address stance should look like.

If you were standing on a railroad track, your feet would be on one track and the ball would be on the other track. So, as you can see, the line of your feet passes to the left of your target, but is not turned to the left.

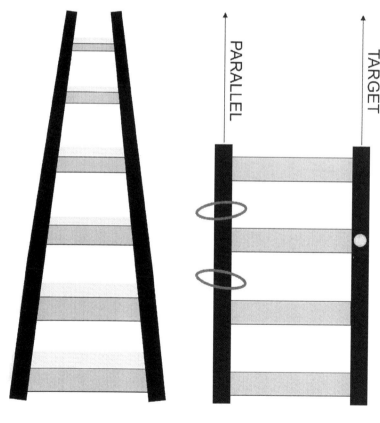

RAILROAD TRACKS   RAILROAD TRACKS

While we are talking about the railroad tracks, if you have ever stood on the tracks and looked down them toward the horizon, the tracks appear to come together. This is what happens to us when we try to line up our shots. So it is important to know your dominate eye, and follow the pre-shot routine related in chapter fourteen.

If you are going to spend sixty minutes a day practicing, then you want to spend at least twenty minutes of that time on putting. Yes, it is that important!

Practicing your chipping techniques can also be fun. Be sure your course has a chipping green, because it is prohibited on most practice putting greens.

First, let's talk about the standard chip shot just off the green, with no object to go over and a clear shot to the pin. It is often call the bump and run. This shot is played back in your stance with about sixty percent of your weight on the left side, and is often played with a seven, eight or nine iron. The easiest way to play the shot is to stroke the ball like a putt. Many players use the putting grip and stance. The ball will come out low with a little top spin and roll out when it hits the green. Practice with all three clubs from different distances in order to know how the ball will react for you.

The bump and run can be played with the ball 'applying the brakes', or checking up, when it hits the green. To do this, everything is the same except use your regular grip and leave your weight evenly distributed, but leaning to your left. On the backswing, break your wrists up as you take the club away and release the wrists down into the back of the ball as you strike it, with a short follow through. The ball must be struck first with nothing between the ball and the club face. When grass gets between the ball and the club face, it is difficult to put spin on the ball.

Photo by Robert "Lumpy" Lumpkin

This is why it is hard to put spin on the ball out of the rough.

The standard pitch shot is played slightly back of center in the stance with weight evenly distributed. This shot should be played with a pitching wedge, thus the name. The natural loft of this club, of approximately forty-eight degrees, allows the ball to ride up the club face, and thus give you a nice high shot.

This shot, if hit cleanly, will give you a little bit of back spin on the ball for some stopping power. If not struck cleanly, it will run, because the back spin is negated by the grass blocking the grooves on the club face. You want to use this shot when you have an object to go over with plenty of green between the object and the hole.

When you have little green between the object to go over and the hole on the green, you should choose a lob shot. A sand wedge is generally used for this type of shot. We have all seen Tiger and Phil make these big swings and pop the ball up in the air. To steal a phrase: The ball lands on the green like a butterfly with sore feet.

However, this big swing technique I do not recommend for amateur golfers, unless you have hours upon hours to practice it. The easier way to play this shot is similar to a greenside bunker shot. Open your stance, aim a little left, open the club face a few degrees, play the ball in the middle of the stance with the weight evenly distributed, and make an upright swing. You will need to practice to see how far the ball will travel in the air with how much effort you give it. All players will hit the ball differently.

Practice putting more weight on the left and the right side to see how the shot reacts. Also practice moving the ball forward and back in your stance, and watch what happens. For most players, the further back in the stance, and the more weight that is on the left, the further the ball will go in the air, albeit a little lower trajectory. Again, if you cannot make clean contact, play for a little run out when the ball hits the green.

This shot is not recommended to be played off a tight lie or hard pan. *However*, with some practice, you can successfully get the ball to pop up and over the object in front of you. All the techniques are the same, except use a pitching wedge, because the sand wedge's leading edge bounce is too much. You must also strike just behind the ball, so your club does not bounce into it. This is a shot that is fun to practice and I recommend that you practice it a lot, because it will help you with the normal lob shot situation, making it easier for you to master the lob.

For all these shots, you must not let the club head pass your lead hand. This can cause you to skull the ball over the green or hit it fat. Either way, it is just luck if it results in a good shot.

Of the sixty minutes of practice time, you should spend ten minutes on all these different types of short game shots. While there, spend another five minutes in the greenside bunker practicing sand shots.

After spending twenty minutes on putting, ten minutes on the short game, five minutes in the bunker, you now have twenty-five minutes left. Go to the range and practice the shots from fifty to one hundred yards for ten minutes. Spend another five minutes on your hybrid, fairway wood clubs and long irons. This will leave you ten minutes to practice working on your driver.

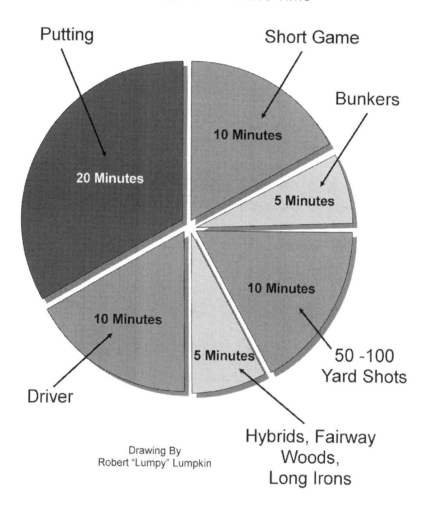

Breakdown Of Where To Spend
60 Minutes Of Practice Time

Putting

Short Game

Bunkers

10 Minutes

20 Minutes

5 Minutes

10 Minutes

10 Minutes

5 Minutes

50 -100
Yard Shots

Driver

Drawing By
Robert "Lumpy" Lumpkin

Hybrids, Fairway
Woods,
Long Irons

No matter what you are going to practice, to get the most of your time, you must practice like you're on the golf course. Picture yourself in a situation where you are going to need the shot that you are working on.

This is so important, because it will accomplish several things. You will be visualizing the shots, developing environmental awareness, putting pressure on yourself, (thus learning how to handle it on the course), building confidence as you succeed better with each shot, and you will be learning your natural tendencies.

Okay, what you've been waiting for, practicing with the driver. I don't know any golfer that does not enjoy hitting the 'Big Dog', including myself. So here is how to get the most out of the practice time.

For every swing you make on the range with your driver, go through the routine that I talk about in chapter fourteen. Spend most of your time working on the inside swing path.

In all likelihood, you have watched the great players on TV when the camera is behind them. Notice how the ball seems to go off the screen to the right. Guess what, the ball *is* taking off to right field. Yes, the convex of the camera lens exaggerates the amount the ball appears to be headed to the right, but this clearly shows the ball is being struck from the inside. Still not convinced? Remember during some of the telecasts the producer has the tracker overlaid on the screen to follow the flight of the ball? The lines also clearly show the ball going out to right field and turning back. Yep, those are draws being hit by those great players!

Next, spend your time on feeling your natural timing, rhythm and tempo. DO NOT care how far the ball goes. I will repeat that. DO NOT care how far the ball goes. Remember, the ball just gets in the way and you need to strike the ball in the center of the club face. If you need a refresher, refer to chapter five and the smash factor.

Over the years, many golfers have asked me how far they should be able to hit their clubs. Every player's distances are different. There is just eight to ten yards difference between clubs. Starting with the five-iron, the average amateur male golfer hits it about one hundred and fifty yards in the air. The average amateur female golfer hits it about one hundred twenty yards in the air. That being the case, the following table illustrates what the average amateur distances are. Also included are the estimated tour pro averages and my yardages. Remember, these are yardages that the ball carries, and does not include any run out after the ball hits the ground.

YARDS IN THE AIR

	MEN	WOMEN	TOUR PRO	LUMPY
DRIVER	220 & UP	180 & UP	280 & UP	260 & UP
3 WOOD	210	170	260	250
5 WOOD	190	160	240	230
3 IRON	170	140	220	210
4 IRON	160	130	210	200
5 IRON	150	120	200	190
6 IRON	140	110	190	180
7 IRON	130	100	180	170
8 IRON	120	90	170	160
9 IRON	110	80	160	150
PITCH W.	100	70	150	140
52 SAND	80	50	140	130
56 SAND	70	40	130	120

Chart By Robert " Lumpy" Lumpkin

During one of my golf schools about five years ago, I had the pleasure of meeting one of the finest couples I have ever had the good fortune to teach. There is no need to mention their names, because they will surely remember this story.

Ah what the heck; might as well publish your picture, M & J, because the readers are going to want to see you after this story. By the way, it should be said here and now, that they are every much the gentleman and lady.

Well, the lady asks me how she would know when she really hit a solid shot on the center of the club face. So I related the lines from a movie about the tuning fork going off in your loins. A few minutes later she nailed a shot down the range. At that particular school, we had twenty students and five professional golf instructors, all on the range at the same time. All the students were practicing diligently on all they had learned over the first two days.

All of a sudden, this lady takes off running around the entire tee box yelling, "Woo-Hoo, Woo-Hoo, the tuning fork went off!" This went on for a couple of minutes, as all the rest of us stopped what we were doing and watched. She was so excited and elated to have been able to feel what a great shot in golf feels like. To this day, they are in my phone directory under: "Woo-Hoo."

What a great couple and patriots. He is a retired Colonel from the Army. M and J, thank you for a fun week and for your friendship over the last several years.

NOTES

~~~~~~~~~~~~~~~~~~~~~

CHAPTER 11
COURSE MANAGEMENT

Course management is probably not taught enough. There are three rules in course management that should *never* be violated. The first is that when in trouble, get out safely. Second one is never try a golf shot on the course that you have not practiced completely and fully. And third, if a layup is called for, make sure you layup with plenty of room to spare.

Quick little story to drive the point home. Sorry about the pun. While I was playing in a professional tour event I drove the ball into the woods off the tee box. Calling it woods is being very polite. My caddy found the ball deep in the jungle. No matter where I looked, the only opening was back towards the tee. Then I spotted a small opening out toward the one hundred fifty yard marker. Yeah, you guessed it, I went for the small opening. After all, I was a professional and could pull off any shot. The ball careening off the tree(s) nearly took my caddy's head off.

Finding way out of woods!?

Now my position was even worse off. Not learning from the first dumb decision, I tried another play in the direction of the green. Again a solid hit, right smack into a tree. Undeterred, I took another approach sideways and buried it in the side of a bush. Unplayable lie would be an understatement, not to mention I was standing in knee deep jungle plants. So you can imagine the drop I got to take.

Finally, I decided that going back toward the tee was a great way to get out of trouble. Two swings later, through the under brush, I arrived safely on the fairway 263 yards to the green. You guessed it again; I pulled out the three-wood and let it rip. Except for the golf gods showing mercy on me, I would have been in the jungle again. Meanwhile, my playing partners had ordered a pizza and some beer.

Finally hitting a wedge onto the back fringe, I took three more shots to get the ball into the hole. Even though it was not as pretty as Tin Cup's twelve, it was a nice one just the same. At the turn my caddy ran into the clubhouse and purchased a can of insect repellant and gave it to me on the next tee. We had a great laugh and went on to post an impressive score of 84. When in trouble, get out safely!

Speaking of a caddy, if you choose to utilize the right to have a guy or gal on your bag, remember you are responsible for all the rules of golf. A few years ago while competing in a tour event in North Carolina I hit an errant shot just out of the rough near an old railroad tie retaining wall. My caddy found the ball against a broken and rotted 'rr-tie', lodged in the mud.

The next shot was great! I pounded it out into the fairway, knocked it on the back fringe, and putted it in for a par. Wow! Walking to the next tee box, my caddy was finally able to clean the ball. Oh, No! It was not my ball. Failing to replay the shot with a penalty, which the rules would have allowed, got me disqualified; to the astonishment of the dozen or so gallery fans that followed me that day.

The caddy felt just awful. However, I made it abundantly clear that it was not her fault…it was mine. The moral here is twofold. You, the player, are responsible for all that happens during your round, and it is in your best interest to *know* the rules!

Rule two: never try a golf shot on the course that you have not practiced completely and fully. I watched in horror as one of my professional playing partners had a nightmare. His ball had ended up on the edge of a greenside bunker. The only shot he had was left handed, if he was going to put the ball on the green. Yes, he could chip it to the fairway, but I guess he reasoned that would add a shot, and he was only ten feet off the green. The ball was in a deep type of buried lie in snarly grass. Nonetheless, he turned his pitching wedge upside down and made the swing. From lying two just ten feet off the green, he went on to card an ugly seven, and only because he got lucky and rolled in a putt from thirty-five feet.

Rule three: if you are going to layup, layup with plenty of room to spare. I have seen so many amateurs make the right decision to layup and then hit it too far into a hazard. There's only eight or ten yards difference between club distances. So if you lay up thirty yards back instead of ten yards, you are only going to have to use two more clubs. The risk of getting closer is not worth it.

Another thing that I have seen quite often is an amateur choosing the wrong club out of a fairway bunker. A few years back I was playing a recreational round of golf with a great group of guys.

My pairing that day put me with one of the higher handicap players. A great guy, but he played a game on the golf course that I did not recognize. Well, he hits his ball into a fairway bunker with a very high lip. A sand wedge was clearly called for. To my astonishment, he walked into the bunker with a four iron.

After hitting the ball three times, and the ball hitting the lip the same number of times, he called me over to give him some advice. He said, and I quote: "Lumpy, I don't understand what's wrong.

I always hit my four iron great," end quote. Spontaneously my other two playing partners began to laugh so hard and loud, he turns to them and says, "What, you guys know I always hit my four iron great!" Now, I kid you not, jokingly I said, "Why don't you just use a 'hand wedge'?" As sober as a judge he says, "I don't think I have one of those in my bag." Bless his heart; he is truly a great guy and a friend to this day.

In a nutshell, course management is using common sense. Sometimes it is the better part of valor to 'bite the bullet' and take your punishment than to go for it. It could just win you a trophy!

NOTES

~~~~~~~~~~~~~~~~~~~~

CHAPTER 12
PROPER ETIQUETTE

Proper etiquette on the golf course is seldom taught, yet it defines who we are with our playing partners. For the most part, etiquette is just being polite and courteous. There are, however, several etiquette specific items that are unique to the game of golf.

To cover the spectrum of proper etiquette that is unique to what takes place on a golf course, it all starts at the bag drop. The bag drop personnel's duties usually extend beyond just loading your bag, but for this purpose, their number one priority is to make you feel welcome and place your bag on the cart in the manner you prefer, irons in or out and who will drive; hopefully someone who won't drive into a lake.

I am often asked what the appropriate tip amount is for the bag drop personnel. Under most circumstances, the industry standard is two dollars per bag. If they are doing a great job, recognize their efforts with a tip amount that you feel is appropriate.

Next, if they are also acting as a starter, they will explain the course regulations, yardage markers, the pin placements, cart path rules for the day and where the rest stops are on the course, as well as any specials at the clubhouse.

As you proceed to your first tee, take note if there are players teeing off. In general, when a player tees off he should be able to reasonably expect to have quiet, so park far enough away so your group can talk but not interfere with the tee box area.

Teeing off on the first tee is generally determined by lot. If continuing a round from a previous day, the player with the lowest score tees off first, then the next best and so on until all players have teed off. As play continues on the course, the player with the best score on the previous hole tees off first, followed in order by the next best score until all players have teed off.

After all players tee off, the player furthest from the hole plays first, then the next furthest away, and so on. In stroke play, there is no penalty for playing out of order, so a lot of groups play 'ready golf'. If you choose to play this way, just make sure there is no one in front of you that could get hit by your flying golf ball. In match play, however, the rules require you to play in order. If you play out of turn, your competitor can require you to cancel your stroke and replay your shot. If you fail to do so, you will lose the hole.

One year in the Solhiem Cup (the ladies' equivalent to the men's Ryder Cup) Anika Sorenstam played out of turn and was required to cancel her stroke and replay the shot. This brought her to tears, because she did not do it on purpose, and had holed out the shot! The rules, however, are the rules, and are there to keep the game fair to all who play.

Once you arrive at the green, the player furthest from the hole still plays first. Now, sometimes it's the player that is on the green, even though another player is in the bunker, because the sand shot is closer to the hole. When you walk onto the green, and the entire time that you are on the green, be aware of where the other players' golf balls are laying. You want to make sure you do not walk on their intended line to the hole, as well as the line extended beyond the hole. So when you mark your ball, do all that you can, not to step in their line.

During a recreational round of golf with some out-of-town friends, one of the golfers in my group was a real rookie in the game of golf. He is a great guy and a hero who risks his life often for his fellow man as a professional firefighter in New York City. However, he had never been taught golf etiquette and did not understand about not walking in the line of someone else's putt. After he walked in my line three or four times, using humor, I politely explained what he was doing. He apologized and was somewhat embarrassed, but did his best the rest of the round to watch for the other players' line of putt. So, if someone walks in your line, just politely point it out to them and I'm sure they will do their best after that.

While on the green, it is customary for the player that is the closest to the hole to tend the flagstick or remove it if no player needs it tended. The player who holes out first should replace the flag after the hole is completed by all the other players. It is also customary for all players to leave the green together.

Some players think it is a violation of the rules of golf to give another player the yardage marker distance that is marked on the golf course. It is understandable because giving another player advice is a violation of the rules. However, providing public information is not a violation of the rules, so next time feel free to let the player know what the yardage marker distance is. This will speed up play, and is the courteous thing to do.

Speed of play is one of the most controversial topics in all of golf. Golf courses recommend that no more than four and one half hours be consumed to complete an eighteen hole round of golf. The general rule of thumb is to stay within sight of the group in front of you. But, if that group is playing slow, it backs up the entire golf course, and no golfer likes to continually wait to hit their next shot. So do your best to play each hole in fifteen minutes or less and you will play in four and a half hours or less. If the group in front of you is playing very fast and you cannot keep up, even though you are playing fifteen minutes a hole, and there is a group behind yours who is always waiting on you, simply let their group play through. This is polite and perfectly acceptable behavior on the links.

Never hit into the players in front of you. Not only is this dangerous, it is extremely poor etiquette. Through the years, because of the length that I could hit a golf ball, some playing partners that I have been paired with would want me to hit into the group to 'send them a message'. The only message this sends is that the person who hit the ball is not wrapped too tight. One of the most ridiculous fights I have ever witnessed was over just this type of behavior. After a player hit into the group in front, one of the players in the forward group hit the ball back. Words were exchanged, and the next thing you know fists were flying.

If you should ever accidentally hit into a group, the proper etiquette is to go to them at the earliest opportunity and apologize.

This can happen because you did not see the players ahead of you over a hill, or in the woods, or for some other reason.

Speaking of being hit accidentally by a golf ball, a few years ago I was retained as an expert witness to investigate what went wrong on a golf course in our nation's capital. A lady was walking down the sidewalk next to a golf course, when whap, a golf ball strikes her in the head.

The day that I arrived to begin the investigation, it was a beautiful sunny day, with several golfers on the course. I was able to observe shots headed in all directions. In this particular case, it did not involve etiquette in the strictest since of the word, however, the design of the tee box actually aimed the golfer at the street. To compound the problem, there was only a six foot chain link fence to stop any golf ball that might go astray. A simple design flaw had caused a nightmare for this lady. Etiquette and common sense would dictate that someone apologize to her, whether the golfer or the golf course. In part, because she was not greeted properly when she complained, it resulted in a lawsuit. After completion and submission of my report, I assume that the case was settled, because I was never called to testify.

Language and actions on the golf course can get quite crude. When a player does not live up to his/her expectations, his/her frustrations can be exhibited in many fashions. Cursing, yelling, throwing and breaking clubs, are just a few of the antics we have all witnessed on the course.

This is of course not proper etiquette, and should be avoided. Always try to act like a lady or gentleman on the golf course.

Repairing the golf course as we play the game is all part of etiquette. When you take a divot, either replace the divot, or if the course has sand on the carts, use it to fill in the divot. On the green, repair not only your ball mark, but a couple of others. Hopefully, you do not visit very many bunkers, but when you do, make sure you rake the sand when you are finished. Taking care of these items is just following the golden rule.

One of the things that Mr. Furgason drilled into my head was to never offer advice to help a player *if he has not asked for any help*. In my profession, this can sometimes be misunderstood.

Just because a player you are playing with, who is a good player, does not offer to help you, it does not mean that he's a jerk. He is simply using good etiquette. If you think you want to help someone because they are really nice, ask them first if they would like a tip. Believe me, it is very easy to make an enemy by offering unwanted advice.

During the President's Cup, I had the great pleasure to meet one of the great ambassadors of golf, and one of the greatest players of all time, Gary Player. Even though he was the Captain of the International Team, he walked frequently outside the ropes with the gallery. For two holes I was honored to talk with him and listen as he talked about the etiquette of golf.

One of the younger American fans got a little carried away rooting for our home team. He made a nasty comment about one of the International players hitting a bad shot. Mr. Player was so polite and kind, but explained that while you can, and should, root for your country, *it is very impolite and bad etiquette to root against the other players.*

If you ever have the opportunity to meet Mr. Player, it will be an experience you will never forget. On behalf of all golfers in America, Mr. Player, let me thank you for setting such a great example for golfers all around the world.

Take the time to read, in its entirety, what the USGA[17] has to say about etiquette in golf. It is Section I in the Rules of Golf. Below is the introduction:

This section provides guidelines on the manner in which the game of golf should be played. If they are followed, all players will gain maximum enjoyment from the game. The overriding principle is that consideration should be shown to others on the course at all times.

Golf is played, for the most part, without the supervision of a referee or umpire. The game relies on the integrity of the individual to show consideration for other players and to abide by the rules. All players should conduct themselves in a disciplined manner, demonstrating courtesy and sportsmanship at all times, irrespective of how competitive they may be. This is the spirit of the game of golf.

17USGA, Liberty Corner Road, Far Hills, NJ
908-234-2300, www.usga.org

NOTES

Chapter 13
Rules Of Golf Commonly Encountered

Every golfer needs to pick up a rule book on the game of golf. The USGA[17] publishes a new and updated book each year. We will not cover all the rules, but briefly touch on rules that you may commonly come across in a normal round of golf. The entire rule is not included here, so consult the rule book for a complete explanation.

Ever hit the ball on the cart path? Yes, you are entitled to relief under Rule 24-2. The player must lift the ball and drop it, without penalty, within one club length of, and not nearer the hole, than the nearest point of relief. Obstructions in the rules of golf are defined as anything artificial, including the artificial surface and sides of roads and paths, etc. The nearest point of relief is defined as the point on the course nearest to where the ball lies that is not nearer the hole, and where, if the ball were so positioned, no interference by the condition from which relief is sought would exist for the stroke the player would have made from the original position, if the condition were not there.

In order to determine the nearest point of relief accurately, the player should use the club with which he would have made his next stroke, if the condition were not there, to simulate the address position, direction of play and swing for such a stroke.

Lifting and marking the ball is covered under Rule 20-1. Players often inquire as to *who* can mark and lift the ball. A ball may be lifted by the player, his partner or another person authorized by the player. In any such case, the player is responsible for any breach of the rules. The ball must be marked before it is lifted under a rule that requires it to be replaced. If it is not marked, the player incurs a penalty of one stroke and the ball must be replaced. If it is not replaced, the player incurs the general penalty of one stroke under this rule, but there is no additional penalty.

A ball to be placed under the rules *must be placed* by the player or his partner. If a ball is to be replaced, the player, his partner or *the person who lifted or moved it must place it* on the spot from which it was lifted or moved. If the ball is placed or replaced by any other person, and the error is not corrected as provided in Rule 20-6, the player incurs a penalty of one stroke.

The position of the ball on the green should be marked by placing a ball marker, small coin or other similar object immediately behind the ball.

If the ball marker interferes with the play, stance or stroke of another player, it should be placed one of more club head lengths to one side. Since the ball on the cart path example is not going to be

replaced, but rather dropped elsewhere, it is acceptable to mark the location of the ball with a tee.

Place Coin Behind Ball

Have you had your ball embedded in the soft ground? Relief is entitled under Rule 25-2. A ball embedded in its own pitch-mark in the ground in any closely mown area, through the green, may be lifted, cleaned and dropped, without penalty, as near as possible to the spot where it lay, but not nearer the hole. 'Closely mown area' means any area of the course, including paths through the rough, cut to fairway height or less.

Several golfers have asked me about tending the flagstick when someone is on or off the green. Rule 17-1 states: before making a stroke from *anywhere* on the course, the player may have the flagstick attended, removed or held up to indicate the position of the hole. See the rule for all the variables.

Another interesting question arises regarding the time a player has to putt in a ball that is overhanging the hole. Rule 16-2 states that a player is allowed enough time to reach the hole, without unreasonable delay, and an additional ten seconds. If the ball does not fall in, then the ball must be tapped in. If too long is taken, then the player is deemed to have holed the ball with the next stroke and must add one stoke. No other penalties apply.

Both aeration holes on the course and on the green can be a problem. A local rule is permitted for lifting, cleaning and dropping the ball for relief from such conditions, without penalty through the green. On the green, the ball may be placed at the nearest point of relief, no nearer the hole. This is allowed under Rule 25, ground under repair, when it is not practical to mark the course.

A local rule is also permitted for unplayable conditions, such as extreme wetness, snow, ice etc., again under Rule 25. Such rule is commonly called 'winter rules' or 'preferred lie'. A ball lying on a closely mown area, through the green, may be lifted without penalty and cleaned. Before lifting the ball, the player must mark its position. Having lifted the ball, he must place it on a spot within one club length of and not nearer the hole than where it originally lay, that is not in a hazard and not on a putting green. A player must mark the ball prior to lifting, and place it only once, or incur a penalty of one stroke.

Relief Permitted With Local Rule

* Photo edited by Robert "Lumpy" Lumpkin

Golfers are often confused about the drop they are entitled if the ball is in a lateral hazard. One of those options is on the other side of the hazard. Lateral hazards are marked with red stakes, while a water hazard is marked with yellow stakes.

This rule does not apply to a water hazard, (yellow stakes) but is an additional option from a lateral hazard.

Rule 26-1c states, as additional options available only if the ball last crossed the margin of a lateral water hazard, drop a ball outside the water hazard within two club-lengths of and not nearer the hole than (i) the point where the original ball last crossed the margin of the water hazard or (ii) *a point on the opposite margin of the water hazard equidistant from the hole.* A ball is considered to be in the lateral water hazard if it lies in or any part of it touches the lateral water hazard.

If the hazard is marked by stakes and or lines, the stakes and the lines are considered to be in the hazard and the outside of the stakes, at ground level, determines the boundary of the hazard. Check out the rule to see what the (i) and (ii) notes allow you to do.

While covering hazards, let's talk about a different kind of hazard, lightning! The USGA emphasizes that players in a competition have the right to stop play if they think lighting threatens them, even though the Committee may not have authorized it specifically by signal. (Rules 6-8 and 33-2d)

Certainly as a golfer, whether competing or not, you should not mess around with the threat of lightning. You should seek shelter in a large permanent building or a fully enclosed metal vehicle (cars, vans, trucks) or the lowest elevation area you can find. Be sure to avoid tall objects (trees/poles), small rain and sun shelters, large open areas, wet areas or elevated areas, all metal objects including: golf clubs, golf carts, fences, electrical and maintenance machinery and power lines.

Many students have asked about removing loose impediments that interfere with putting from the fringe. Rule 23-1 states: except when both the loose impediment and the ball lie in or touch the same hazard, any loose impediment may be removed without penalty.

Here, however, is the rub. You *may not* remove sand anywhere on the course *except* on the putting green! I see players all the time brush away sand that has been splashed out from a greenside bunker.

The rule book defines loose impediments as natural objects including: stones, leaves, twigs, branches and the like, dung, worms, insects and the like, and the casts and heaps made by them; provided they are not fixed or growing, solidly embedded or adhering to the ball. *Sand and loose soil are loose impediments on the putting green, but not elsewhere.*

So, the next time you have sand on the fringe, resist the urge to remove the sand or loose soil, because it is a two stroke penalty infraction under the rules of golf.

Another often asked question that golfers have is whether their ball is on the green or the fringe when it is partially touching the fringe? The rules of golf clearly states that if any part of the ball touches the putting green, it is on the green and you can, therefore, mark, lift and clean the ball.

In the chapters on etiquette and playing competitive golf, I talk about giving your competitive playing partner information that is on the yardage marker and that it is *not* considered to be advice. The definition of advice under the rules of golf is any counsel or suggestion that could influence a player in determining his play, the choice of a club or the method of making a stroke. Information on the rules, *distance* or matters of public information, such as the position of hazards or the flagstick on the putting green, *is not advice*.

Numerous golfers have asked why there is not a rule governing slow play. Well, there is, and it is Rule 6-7 which states: the player must play without undue delay and in accordance with any pace of play guidelines that the Committee may establish. Between completion of a hole and playing from the next teeing ground, the player must not unduly delay play. In match play, the penalty is loss of hole, and in stroke play it is a two stoke penalty.

For the purpose of preventing slow play, the Committee may, in the conditions of a competition (Rule 33-1), establish pace of play guidelines including maximum periods of time allowed to complete a stipulated round, a hole or a stroke.

In stroke play only, the Committee may, in such a condition, modify the penalty for a breach of this rule as follows: first offense a one stroke penalty, second offense a two stroke penalty and for a subsequent offense a disqualification.

The problem we have with the slow play rule on public golf courses is that there is not an official golf competition taking place, and, therefore, no committee to enforce the rule.

So, theoretically the golf course becomes the committee and has, in almost all cases, established a four and one half hour time limit to play eighteen holes of golf. Most golf courses have rangers to try to keep the pace of play moving along. But what can a golf course do to penalize slow play? Nearly any option that golf courses have at their discretion risks alienating their customer, the golfer.

So my fellow golfers, it is up to us to ensure we do our part to play within the stipulated time frame, and to spread the word to all golfers courteously and politely.

I realize reading the rules of golf can be quite dry. But it is in your best interest to familiarize yourself with the rules. The rules are there to help you and to make the game fair for all who play.

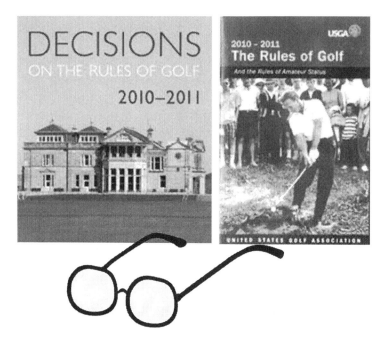

17USGA,
Liberty Corner Road, Far Hills, NJ
908-234-2300, www.usga.org

NOTES

~~~~~~~~~~~~~~~~~~~~

CHAPTER 14
PLAYING COMPETITIVE GOLF

If you are a golfer who enjoys playing in competitive amateur golf events, or would like to start, let me share some insights that I have gained over the years.

Being asked to be the official professional golf instructor for the Grand Strand section of the Golf Channel Amateur Tour, was an honor and pleasure. During that time of helping players, it became apparent that some players had limited competitive experience. Unfortunately, the only way you get experience is to play. However, there are certain things you can do to prepare yourself for competition.

First, get with, and stay with, an instructor that you believe in and trust. Make sure you find an instructor that understands playing and competing under pressure.

After awhile, the instructor will begin to learn your tendencies and know your swing. This is very important, because you cannot see your own swing, but staying with the same instructor makes it easier for him to help you.

Taking lessons on a regular basis also gives you confidence in your swing and a support system. When you are competing, it is easy to lose your confidence, but with the comforting words from your instructor in your head, you are more easily able to stay focused.

Besides myself, I recommend professional golf instructors Mike Schroder[4], and John Robinson[8].

Mike played the 'Big Show' and has his own TV instructional golf show "Links Illustrated" that is aired on family and sports channels. He has also produced a great video called 'Simplify Your Golf Game,

By Knowing Your Style and Tendencies', and has a great golf learning complex.

John is both an amateur and professional champion. He won the All Central Indiana UAW Amateur Championship and won four tournaments on the Sunbelt Senior Professional Golf Tour. John has a fantastic home golf facility with all the amenities.

Practice is the next most important thing you must do, both mental and physical. Refer to the chapter on practicing and stay consistent in your practice time.

If you are going to compete, you must play a lot of golf, and stay under the tutelage of an experienced pro. One of the things we have discussed is to accept your environment. The best way to accomplish this is to make the golf course a home away from home. The more time you spend in an environment, the more likely you are to be relaxed and comfortable.

Imagine for a moment, if you had to go to an unfriendly foreign country and find a lost loved one, and *you have never been to that environment*. So, you need to find someone who has, and seek their advice. Who would you seek out to help you? Rambo comes to mind, and the reason is that you want someone with experience who has been thoroughly trained in the environment. Get the idea? Get with, and stay with a pro with the experience to help you, and spend a lot of time on the course, the competitive environment.

Relaxing on the golf course is imperative to playing competitive golf. Your muscles cannot function properly if they are tense. This, of course, directly affects your golf swing, and particularly your timing, rhythm and tempo.

Next, you need to look forward to competing. I have read about famous pros that would get very sick and nauseous before they teed off. Despite this, they had an intense desire to compete.

How a player handles his nerves can vary greatly between each individual. You will, however, be required to do so if you are going to compete. One of the ways is to put the competition in proper prospective. Count your many blessings and be happy and content that you have the ability and 'where-with-all' to enjoy doing something you truly want to do.

You must remain 'golf physically fit' and flexible. This is one of the biggest reasons that, at my age, I can still put the ball out there pretty well. I can still stand with my knees locked and bend over and lay my hands flat on the ground, as well as still able to connect my fingers together behind my back, with the over and behind arm stretch. You know the importance of stretches and fitness that was discussed in chapter nine.

You must develop a pre-shot routine that you use for every shot. This helps prepare you to do something that you do all the time. Get with your instructor, and he or she can share some specific actions you can do for your particular swing. My pre-shot routine is simple, but effective for me. You are welcome to give it a try.

The first thing to do is get the correct yardage: front, center and back of green. Then fix your mind on where you want the ball to go, and pick a specific target in the distance, <u>that is not on the ground</u>. Pick a tall branch on a tree in the background or perhaps the top of a chimney on a house in the distance.

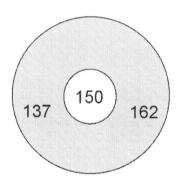

Once you have selected the club for the correct yardage, line up your shot from behind the ball and pick something laying on the ground, a foot or so in front of the ball that is line with your intended target. It is easier to line up to something a foot away than something several yards away.

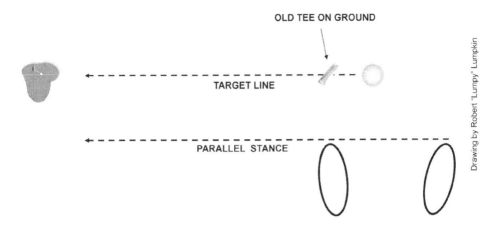

Hold your club up and use it as a straight edge to line up the object in front of the ball and the intended target. Walk up to the side of the ball and make a practice swing over the top of the ball. This is important, because as the club passes over the ball, you can see the club swing on an inside path. As you address the ball, say to yourself "relax", and take a deep breath and exhale.

Clear your mind of everything except your intended target, step up to the ball, and just swing. Give no thought to the results. Accept whatever happens, and go forward to play your next shot.

As you go to the next shot, do not think about what you are going to do until you get there. Then go through the same routine again.

When you play, you will have a better chance of playing well if you just swing and trust that natural swing that is within you. My experience is that I play my best when I swing like I don't care. Yes, of course I care, and take the time to line up and keep the same swing routine. But the truth is, I know I will hit a better shot without caring about the results!

Let me share this story with you. Many years ago I was trying to qualify for a state open competition. My tee time was not until two in the afternoon, so I decided to get some practice in on the golf course. By the rules, I could not play a practice round at the venue site, so I went to a local public links with a friend of mine.

My round of golf was just horrible. I was mentally trying to remember all the things my instructor had told me, and was trying very hard to hit good shots. The result was a devastating score of ninety-one. It seemed impossible, because my average score was seventy-three. How in the world was it possible to shoot that high of a score? Even worse, the venue course was much more difficult. A decision had to be made. Should I withdraw from the qualifier or go and be totally embarrassed. To add even more pressure, my instructor was scheduled to caddy for me.

Well, I decided to go, but on my drive there it became clear that I could not do worse than just playing like I <u>did</u> <u>not</u> <u>care</u>. So, when the tee time finally arrived, it was now or never to just trust my swing and play like there was no concern in the world about the results.

To my amazement, I was five under par with three holes to play. The zone that was being experienced was surreal. However, realizing that *something special was going on* caused me to start thinking again; I went on to bogey two of the last three holes. Luckily, shooting a sixty-nine still qualified.

Another thing you need to prepare yourself for is an adrenaline rush. This can cause a rapid heartbeat, nausea, headache and a myriad of other confusing things to the person who has never experienced it before. In my case, I thought I was having a heart attack. Wow, what an experience! So, if it happens to you, just relax and realize that it is a normal physiological occurrence and don't panic; it will pass. <u>A word of caution is called for here</u>, since I am not a physician. If you think there is a medical problem, seek immediate medical assistance.

A few years back I was playing in a professional tour event on the Sunbelt Senior Professional Golf Tour[3]. The title sponsor is now Cancun, and the presenting sponsor is Palace Resorts. It is the longest running mini-tour in the country and was founded by a great guy, Don Barnes, with the assistance of his good friend and Professional Golfer, the late Joe Kriznuski. By the way, amateurs forty-seven and older are welcome to play on the tour, and I encourage you to contact

Mr. Barnes and compete in some events. The tour also has pro-am competitions and you can play golf with some of the best pros around.

Well, Mr. Barnes wanted to help me and referred me to a swing and mental guru. The guru had played on the 'Big Show' tour and was well known. After some discussion, I retained him to help me.

It was one of my better decisions. Some of what I'm about to share, came from him. Unfortunately he passed away and my heart goes out to his family.

When you compete, you must remember that the only thing that changes from the range to the first tee is the environment. Let's repeat that. When you compete, you must remember that the only thing that changes from the range to the first tee is the environment. You still have the same swing and abilities; you've just changed location/environment.

The same is true of playing with your weekend group or in a tournament. If you are going to compete, always play by the rules that you have to play by in competition. Again, the more you do the same thing, the more likely you are to be comfortable in the situation and environment.

In order to compete successfully, you must conquer your fear of hitting a bad shot. Learning to accept the results is the first step. You must also have confidence in recovering from any situation you find yourself in.

Never be discouraged by a bad round of golf when you are competing, especially if you are trying to achieve something, which in your life, is a big thing to do. A perfect example is in 2004, I tried to qualify for the U. S. Senior Open. The below [14]article was published on the internet, for all to see, with my name coming up on the search.

Jul 1, 2004 ... The Boscobel Golf Club professional used steady play and nine hole scores of 34 – 36 to .... Robert Lumpkin (Little River, SC), 39, 42, 81 ...
USGA - United States Senior Open – Qualifying
Greenwood Country Club – Greenwood, SC. July 1, 2004

With soggy conditions and a never ending chance of rain, Terry Mauney of Charlotte, NC shot a 4-under par 68 to take home medalist honors.

Mauney got off to a great start-making birdie on the first hole, a 500-yard par five, and another birdie on the dangerous par four, number four. His lone bogey of the day came on the par five sixth hole and there were no mistakes after that. Mauney birdied holes eight, nine, and thirteen and made pars everywhere else to shoot nines of 33 – 35 for his qualifying score of 68.

Taking the second qualifying spot was Mike Hamilton of Simpsonville. The Boscobel Golf Club professional used steady play and nine hole scores of 34 – 36 to finish at two under par 70. The third and final spot didn't come so easily. Greenville native, Frank Wrenn battled through a five man, four hole playoff making birdie on hole thirteen to advance the Championship.

Four alternates for the Sr. Open were determined from this qualifier, all of which came in a playoff. Taking these alternate spots were: first with a par on his fourth playoff hole was Gary Brown of Charlotte, NC, 2nd Frank Ford from Charleston, SC, 3rd Ted Padgette of Hollywood, SC and the final spot was won by Cliff SeastrunkofRaleigh,NC. The 2004 US Senior Open Championship will be played at Bellerive Country Club located in St. Louis, MO. The 2004 field will consist of both exempt players and players qualifying at their regional sites. This US Senior Open qualifier is one of 9 USGA qualifiers conducted by the South Carolina Golf Association[14]. -End of Article-

As you can see, not a stellar round of golf, and missed the Open by ten shots. What you have to take from this is the great satisfaction that you were there competing to go to one of the greatest events in golf. *So never ever be embarrassed or discouraged by the results.*

Yes, I went on to playing better rounds in the Open Qualifier, but never qualified. If memory serves me correctly, I think the best I ever did was come within four shots. The competition, however, was worth it all. So remember, *the only ones who do not fail, are the ones who do not compete.* I have had my fair share of great rounds of golf in the sixties for this very reason. All golfers shoot high scores, even the great players we have discussed in this book. If any golfer tells you that he or she never played a bad round, they are being less than honest with you.

Finally, make time on a daily basis to find a quiet place to be alone with your thoughts. Visualize playing a perfect round of golf in your mind. The more specific you can be about the round, the better. Several years ago I read a self-help book, (wish I could remember the title), which talked about the power of the mind. One of the examples given was about a prisoner of war who, for five years, did nothing in his quiet time but visualize himself bowling a perfect score.

When he was finally released and returned to the states, he went bowling. You guessed it; he bowled a perfect three hundred.

You have nothing to lose, and everything to gain by spending some quiet time just imagining the perfect round of golf! This is also one of the programs that the guru put me on. It does work, and you will be glad that you spent the time and effort on it.

As you visualize, see the shot flying to the green and landing just where you intended. See yourself making the putt, and feel the pleasure that naturally comes from the unique sound the golf ball makes going into the bottom of the cup. Yes, use all your senses to make the experience as real as possible.

If, during the process, you see a bad shot in your mind, replay the shot in your mind until you have it correct. In my experience, you are going to find this to be more difficult than you may think! Work on all these things, and go enjoy competing!

NOTES

CHAPTER 15
JUNIOR GOLF

The important thing to remember about your children playing golf is that golf is a game. If you try to make your kids develop too quickly, it can be very harmful to their mental and physical success in golf. This does not mean to avoid encouraging them to do their best; simply allow them the same growth opportunities you allow them in other areas.

When your child wants to play golf, do not make the mistake of cutting down an old set of adult clubs. Take the time to research the proper set of junior clubs for your child's age and size. Take into consideration that if they are just beginning, an inexpensive set of junior clubs will work just fine, if the right size and weight.

What you do need to invest in, if he or she shows a real liking for the game, are some golf lessons. The least expensive way to do this is to locate a good junior clinic in your area that is conducted by a certified professional who enjoys working with kids.

A County Wide Junior Clinic
Conducted by Robert "Lumpy" Lumpkin

We care about children, so their faces have been intentionally blurred for their protection.

To give you an idea of just how talented some children can be, I would like to share the following article with you, which was recently published in a local newspaper. To say it was a pleasure to work with this young man would be an understatement. He is currently using his talents in other sports as well. I wish him all the success his young life has before him.

North Myrtle Beach youth golfer is chasing golf pro Tiger Woods
By Elsa Bonstein, correspondent

I had the most extraordinary experience last week. I think I saw a future champion.

His name is Hunter Green. He is 7 years old with longish blond hair, a killer grin and a golf swing for which I would give my eyeteeth.

It all started when the Beacon got a tip about a kid in North Myrtle Beach who is a golf phenomenon, shooting 34-38 on nine-hole par-3 courses down there. I made a few phone calls, and last Thursday I drove down to Black Bear Golf Course on S.C. 9 in Longs and met Hunter, his grandmother and his coach.

Hunter was hitting balls on the practice tee when I got there. I watched as he hit ball after ball, each one perfectly straight and out about 130 yards or more.

I asked his coach, Robert (Lumpy) Lumpkin of U.K. Golf and the Getaway Golf Academy at Black Bear, if Hunter could hit short irons, chip shots and sand wedges. The big guy kind of smirked at me, walked over to Hunter, put down a ball and handed his protégé a 9-iron.

"Hunter? You see that shadow right out there in line with that tree?"

Hunter nodded.

"Can you hit the ball there?"

Hunter took a stance, whaled the ball and it flew up high and true, then landed smack dab in the middle of the shadow.

Lumpy told him to hit a half shot just down to the bottom of the hill. He did.

Then Lumpy pushed a ball into the sand, handed him the sand wedge and bingo, the ball flew up like a frightened bird.

Wow! I was a believer.

Hunter came to live with his grandmother, Teresa Stover, in North Myrtle Beach when he was six weeks old. Today she is "Ma" to him in everything he does.

"Hunter was a blessing to me from the start," Teresa said. "I had lost my mother shortly before he came, and it was almost like she sent him to me so I wouldn't be alone."

Hunter was a regular kid until one day when he was 18 months old.

"I went to the Wal-Mart and Hunter picked up a toy golf club and started swinging it. He seemed to enjoy it, so I bought it for him and he started hitting balls all over the place. He wore out the first club, and I bought him a second one. Pretty soon balls were bouncing off walls and flying into neighbors' yards.

"I showed him the Golf Channel on TV, and pretty soon he was watching it all the time."

Teresa doesn't play golf, and doesn't know why Hunter wants golf more than anything else. "He just wanted to play golf from the time he was a toddler."

Teresa tried to hook Hunter up with a teacher of golf, but most pros did not want to work with a kid that young. Along the way, he did have a few lessons and got some cut-down adult clubs.

Finally, Hunter matched up with Lumpy.

"I heard about the kid and was willing to work with him," Lumpy explained. "He looked amazing to me from the start. I put him on my golf simulator at the U.K. Golf facility, and his swing matched Tiger Woods within a few degrees.

"I've had him out on the course and at various golf facilities, and Hunter has an amazing ability to mimic other players. This can be good or bad because if he sees a guy hitting the ball with a big loop at the top of his swing, Hunter can do that too.

"I try to explain the cause and effect of different kinds of swings, and he understands."

While we were talking, Hunter was hitting balls, and then he was running around the back of the practice area and up to the clubhouse. He seemed like a very active child.

"He's a good student," Teresa said. "He does well in school. Last year he played T-Ball and hit home runs, way out there, probably because of all his practice at golf."

Patrick Wilkinson, the general manager of Black Bear Golf Course, has arranged for Hunter to have unlimited access to the driving range and the course.

Thanks to Lumpy, Hunter has his own youth golf clubs.

"Having a small kid hit balls with cut-down adult clubs is not good," said Lumpy. "They're heavy, the shafts are too stiff. Hunter needs clubs that fit his size, that have the flex for his swing."

I talked directly with Hunter to find out what this is really all about from his eyes.

"I can't ever remember not playing golf," he told me. "I've just always played."

How often does he play golf or practice?

"Just once a day," he said solemnly.

What courses does he play?

"Possum Trot and Azalea Sands and Black Bear. I hit a ball on Possum Trot right across the water, up to the hole and I sank the putt for a birdie!" He almost levitated with joy of it all.

What's his favorite food? "Watermelon."

His "Ma" explained that Hunter broke the femur on his right arm last spring when he fell off his scooter.

"It was a bad break and needed some work, and when it was all over, he wanted watermelon. The nurses were surprised. Not ice cream or candy, but watermelon."

Hunter has trouble finding kids his age who play golf. Right now, he has two golfing friends, Seth (age 10) and Jason (age 6). Another problem is finding venues for him to compete in. Many junior golf tournaments do not take kids this young.

"Plus, many junior events are in central or western North and South Carolina. They're expensive and require an overnight stay," Teresa said.

How far will Hunter go in the world of golf?

"We want him to go as far as he wants," Lumpy said. "We're here to help and support him."

"I'll never force him to play. It's got to be his decision," echoed Teresa.

"Watch out, Tiger. I'm hunting for you," said Hunter.

~~~~~End of Article~~~~~

For all you parents who want to know more about competitions, the following information is provided by the American Junior Golf Association[12]. The information is excellent and is well worth reading and understanding, especially if your child has the potential to play high school and possibly college golf.

Junior Clinic 9 Hole Competition Day
Conducted by Robert "Lumpy" Lumpkin
We care about children, so their faces have
been intentionally blurred for their protection.

-----ARTICLE-----

How many times have you heard adults say, "I wish I would have started at his age?" Learning the game of golf at a young age is obviously a good thing and playing good golf at a young age is even better. The question for many parents is whether their child is just a good player, or does that child have a chance to be a great player. Recognizing a junior golfer's potential isn't easy, especially if the parents aren't golfers themselves.

The first thing to remember, before we even talk about a child's potential, is encouragement. All juniors start golfing because someone encourages them to play the game. It may be a parent, friend or coach.

This encouragement, along with access to clubs and a course, is the key. So remember to encourage the junior throughout his or her career.

When looking for potential in junior golfers, you have to remember that each junior is going to grow and learn at different rates. Some junior golfers don't score as well simply because they can't hit the ball as far as other kids their age. Many times that's just because they're physically smaller.

So when you're looking for your child's potential at a young age, don't just look at their scores. Watch how they play the game, see how they chip and putt, and look at their shot selection.

A short-hitting junior usually has a pretty good short game. They realize they can't hit as far as the rest of the players their age, but they have also figured out that they can make up for it by chipping and putting well.

Many juniors understand the game instantly, while most kids are just trying to hit the ball as far as they can. That is a sign of real potential.

As a junior golfer gets older, tournaments become more important, whether it's the junior championship at your club or an AJGA (American Junior Golf Association) tournament.

This is where it's very important for parents to encourage and not push. Ultimately it has to be the junior's decision to play, and not the parents' decision. We've all heard the horror stories about the parents who push too hard, and the kids who simply put their clubs in the closest never to play again.

Even with that said, one of the only ways to see how much potential a player has is for that golfer to play against his or her peers. Parents should encourage them to play in as many events as possible *if that's what they want to do.* Remember, a child being nervous before a tournament is normal, dreading going to the tournament is not.

Potential to be a good golfer begins to show at these small events. If the junior does well and likes it, the potential is there. Many good golfers are not tournament players. The stress of competitions is not for everyone. We see that at every level.

With some success at smaller events, the next step is a bigger

bigger tournament. Your city or county is likely to have a junior event where your junior can play against the better kids in the area.

With success in these regional tournaments, you probably have a good player on your hands. If they can finish top 10 in one of these events they can probably play pretty well at the high school level. One thing to remember is that finishing in the top 10 in a golf event in Bangor, Maine, is different than the same finish in Orlando, Florida. Try to be realistic about how much talent was at the event.

The next step is high school golf. If your junior is the No. 1 player on his or her high school team, they probably have a shot at playing at the collegiate level. If your child's high school tournament scoring average is in the low 70s, colleges will find them. If your child has a high school tournament scoring average in the low 80s, they will have to find the college, but there is still a place to play.

For golfers in high school that shoot in the 70s, there are many national junior golf tournament associations. This is where they need to be playing in order to try to reach their true potential[12].

<center>~~~~~End of Article~~~~~</center>

Lumpy's Grandson
Early Signs Of A
Good Swing

Lumpy's
Granddaughter

NOTES

~~~~~~~~~~~~~~~~~~~~

CHAPTER 16
LADIES GOLF

Physically, men and women are built differently. Now there's a big surprise, huh? In my opinion, too much is made of the differences. Let's briefly touch upon what can be a sensitive subject. Yes, it is true that large busted woman adjust their arm swing somewhat; however, I have never seen a woman who does not already understand this, and who does not automatically make the adjustment.

Unless a lady specifically asks me about this subject, I never bring it up when teaching golf, because it is unnecessary. But ladies, if you have a question about this subject relating to your golf swing, by all means do not be bashful about asking your professional golf instructor. You should expect a polite and dignified answer that does not in anyway embarrass you.

There are, however, two swing faults I often see that are common to ladies, including my own beautiful lady. On the backswing, rather than turning their shoulders, ladies have a tendency to turn just enough to allow them to lift their arms up almost immediately. The second common swing fault is, rather than a rotation of the hips, the hips are tilted laterally, causing the loss of posture and a myriad of other swing problems.

The next picture shows the correct and the incorrect way to rotate the hips and lift the arms. Notice the difference in the tilt, the turning of the shoulders, and the rotating hips, all indicated by the white lines. The photo on the left is turning the back to the target, while the photo on the right shows the tilting, rather than turning of the hips.

Correct   Incorrect

Ladies are generally not physically as strong as men. Therefore it is extremely important that you have golf clubs that are designed for women. The difference is a lighter grip, shaft and club heads, allowing you to swing with the same effortless timing, rhythm and tempo as men. Just watch the great ladies on TV, and you will see some of the most rhythmic swings in all of golf. In fact, men can learn a lot by watching these great lady golfers' swings.

So ladies, take your time and shop around to find the correct clubs for you, and the fitting professional that is knowledgeable about women's clubs.

After you have properly fitted clubs, spend some time with a teaching professional. When you inquire about lessons, be sure to confirm that the professional customarily teaches women. This is important to you so you can progress as quickly as possible.

If you are just beginning to play golf, a great way to start is to join into a women's only clinic. It is great socializing and a lot of fun. You will also feel less intimated when you first start playing. I have found, in my experience, it is important for woman to have other ladies to socialize and participate with.

Ladies Golf Clinic
Conducted by:
Robert "Lumpy" Lumpkin

I have included a recent article which I came across while researching this very topic. The following published article, by John Paul Newport, was on the internet about this interesting subject. I have reproduced it here unedited except for the removal of the pictures that were included in the article. I think you will enjoy what some of the ladies have to say.

~~~~~~~~~~~~~~~ARTICLE~~~~~~~~~~~~~~~~

GETTING WOMEN INTO THE GAME
With Participation Stalled, Groups Try New Initiatives; Finding 'Mommy Time'

By JOHN PAUL NEWPORT

Heidi Tobias, a spunky 37-year-old online consultant to small businesses and nonprofits, has had a longstanding interest in golf, primarily because so many people she knows play the game and love to talk about it. She had played field hockey and figured, "I can do this. I can bust into this old boys' club." So three years ago she signed up with a girlfriend (who unfortunately later had to bail) for a one-day, soup-to-nuts golf clinic, which included a set of clubs for her to keep.

She wasn't daunted by being the only female in the clinic. "I'm used to hanging out with guys," she said. "But I walked away saying, 'Whoa! What did you say?'" Too much information, too quickly. Moreover, she didn't know any other beginners, in particular female beginners, with whom to pursue the game further. Her only subsequent golf activity was a round with her fiancé during which, as a joke, she played a few holes with a sign pinned to her back that read, "Play through. She's new."

Last Friday, however, she and another girlfriend attended a more laid-back golf clinic for women, topped off by a wine tasting, which has rekindled her excitement about the game. "We had a great time. There wasn't any big agenda except just to have fun and hit some balls and do a little networking." She and several other women from the event have already arranged to take a series of follow-up lessons together.

The event was sponsored by Women On Course, a three-year-old organization that takes a subtly different approach to connecting women with golf than do more traditional programs. The emphasis is on what founder Donna Hoffman calls the "golf lifestyle" rather than on instruction or the benefits of using golf as a business tool.

This orientation coincides with a growing recognition that the golf industry's efforts to attract and retain women players have not been very successful. The number of female golfers has remained flat in recent years, around 23% of all golfers, while the percentage of rounds played by women over 18 has actually fallen, to 15% from 18% a few years ago, according to National Golf Foundation figures. (Rounds for girls have risen slightly.)

Nancy Berkley, a leading consultant and writer on women's golf issues, believes the game has been pitching itself to women in the wrong way. "It's a 99% male-dominated industry, to start with," she said. "And the emphasis has always been on selling products, mostly to men, more than on marketing the game itself. You can't scold the companies. It's worked for their bottom lines, because most golfers are men. But if you want to attract more women players, golf has to deliver a message that resonates better with women."

GUIDELINES FOR 'WOMEN FRIENDLY' FACILITIES

The Executive Women's Golf Association publishes a set of guidelines for facilities that want to earn official status as "women friendly." Those suggestions include:

- A staff, including at least 10% women, that has a consistent approach to all players regardless of gender, from the pro shop to the bag staff and the marshals
- Equal services provided to men and women. If club fitting is offered, fitters that are well trained to fit equipment for women with equipment available for women golfers of various skill levels. If clothing is sold, an adequate selection of women's clothing in a variety of styles and sizes.
- At least two sets of tees rated for women. The first set should be between 4,600 and 5,300 yards, and the second between 5,300 and 5,800 yards. Courses get extra credit for having a third set of rated tees 5800 yards or longer.
- Carries from the forward tees limited to 50 yards or less for the majority of holes.
- Slope and rating data and course handicap conversion tables for women available in an obvious and easily accessible area.
- Distance markers inside 100 yards.
- Facilities that are relatively equal for men and women, including tee boxes maintained in equal condition and with similar basic amenities (like ball washers and trash cans).
- Clean pleasant restrooms at least every six holes on the course.
- Access for women to any area of the facility except men's locker rooms.

--John Paul Newport

That message, in her view, would focus on golf's health benefits and the sense of physical well-being it engenders, as well as on its social and emotional satisfactions. "Golf is such a great game for women. Nothing beats being outdoors with good friends on beautiful day. But women aren't hearing that," she said.

Ms. Berkley, a longtime devotee of the game and chairman of the golf committee at her club in Florida, recognizes that many women are competitive about golf in the way men more typically are. "But most women in my experience aren't looking for intense competition in the two to four hours they may have free. They're looking for something else, something that has more personal meaning."

Ms. Hoffman, a 50-year-old former TV producer who lives near Washington, arrived at roughly the same place through personal experience. A self-described "single mom" golf widow in her first marriage, she got hooked on the game after taking a golf trip with her second husband, a three-handicapper. "A lot of women never consider golf because they don't understand its benefits," she said. They schedule lunch dates, join book clubs and go to yoga classes and job-related networking events because they enjoy the contact with other women and believe they are getting something substantive from the experiences. "But golf offers the same things, if they only knew it. The most important thing at our events is being with other women, not the golf itself. The golf is something for them to bond around and have fun together with and use to de-stress."

Of the 55 women at last week's Women on Course event, 14 were "never-ever" beginners who first received some basic information about the rules and etiquette of golf (importantly including advice on what to wear) and then a bit of instruction. "It's way harder than it looks," said Allison Queensborough, a 29-year-old working mother of two who was in the beginner's group. "But the teachers were great. They took their time and when we went out to hit balls, I felt very comfortable. It was really fun." So was the extended wine-and-cheese portion of the festivities afterward. Ms. Queensborough and some friends from the event plan on following up with lessons, probably twice a month. A year from now, she said, she hopes they will have improved enough to play occasional nine-hole rounds. "This is going to be something for me, Mommy time, away from the kids and my husband," she said.

The oldest women's-golf group, the 18,000-member Executive Women's Golf Association, is evolving in the same direction. As part of a rebranding this year, it changed its vision statement from "The premier force promoting women's golf" to the more touchy-feely "Enriching the lives of women through the game of golf." In 1991, when the EWGA got started, "the hot-button issue was, how can golf help women break through the glass ceiling? Now it's more about, what are women getting from golf?" said Pam Swensen, the group's chief executive.

Some EWGA chapters are huge (the largest has 900 members) and provide opportunities to compete all the way to an annual national tournament. But the bread-and-butter mission of the organization, Ms. Swensen said, is to "cultivate a warm, nurturing atmosphere for women to become engaged with golf" and to connect them with other women.

June, in case you missed the memo, is American Express Women's Golf Month, an initiative co-sponsored by the EWGA, the PGA of America and other organizations. An online listing of golf facilities offering special, often-free introductory programs for women is available through playgolfamerica.com. Some sound terrific. The kickoff extravaganza Wednesday in Kansas City, Mo., drew 274 women; the lineup at PGA Golf Club in Port St. Lucie, Fla., includes cocktail receptions and pro-shop discounts. But other listings are so sparse as to be laughable, such as free 10-minute lessons between 5 p.m. and 6 p.m., on Thursdays only, at a course in Denver. As if that's really going to bring women into the game.

For all the golf industry's good intentions, the biggest barrier now to women's involvement is probably the same as it's always been: the general sense of intimidation and outsider-ness that women experience at many, but by no means all, golf facilities. But that's a topic for another column.

— Email me at golfjournal@wsj.com.

~~~~~~~~~~~~~~~~End of article~~~~~~~~~~~~~~

Having the chance to develop golf programs for ladies, I have seen many of the things discussed in the article by Mr. Newport. Playing for many years on all types of golf courses, I have heard repeatedly that woman play slowly. This is such non-sense that I feel obligated to set the record straight. Come on guys, we all know we have been behind slow groups, of both men and women. To categorize all women golfers as slow is simply unfair.

Another subject that is often discussed is about couples playing golf together. What a great concept! If you are fortunate enough to have a lady who loves golf as much as you do, then you should embrace the idea and have fun with a regular day of golf with this great lady.

About at this moment, my lady, Beth, is screaming at me to get my clubs and take her golfing. Yes, guys and gals, I, too, fall down in this area, but I have committed to schedule more golf with the most beautiful woman and love of my life. Because after all, it's not only a way to enjoy each other's company, but also an opportunity to get exercise together.

Dedicated to The love of my life, Beth

Word of caution here! Guys do not try to be your lady's instructor. And ladies, give him a break and don't be so hard on him when he offers a tip or two. Ok, I admit that I'm not a marriage counselor, but trust me on this one guys, let her find a professional golf instructor and learn in her own way and at her own pace. The both of you will be glad you did.

If it is possible to get another couple to play as a group, it can be even more fun. I know several couples that do this and have a great time.

But whether you do or not, enjoying each other's company after the round of golf over lunch and some beverages can be rewarding in and of itself.

So grab your clubs and head out to the golf course, relax and have a great time playing golf together.

After the day on the links and a few beverages, continue your time together and enjoy a relaxing sunset together. Ah... the romantic in me comes out. God bless and great golfing!

NOTES

~~~~~~~~~~~~~~~~~~~~

CHAPTER 17
SENIOR GOLF

What exactly defines the age of a senior? Well, in golf it has been defined by the professional tour as fifty years of age. Just recently I was told of a dating service that advertized "if you're 40 and would like to meet other seniors…" Social Security begins at age sixty-two. Others say it is when your junk mail contains a membership offer from AARP. Still others contend that if you're a baby boomer *you are* a senior.

Or if you have a passel of grandchildren like I do, you can pretty much accept the fact that you are a senior. Yep, I have six: Audrey, Mason, Eli, Will, Henry and Coralee.

So you can pick the age and decide, but if you ever played with one of these wagons or other pictured toys, or recognize some of the pictures in this chapter, you are most likely a senior.

But in golf, if you are fifty or older you qualify as a senior. I'm not sure when the "Up Tees" got classified as senior tees, but just because you are fifty does not mean you should play those tees.

Here is a good criterion for you to use to determine the tee box that is appropriate for you to play. Choose the tee box that allows you to get close to the one hundred and fifty yard area off the tee, on normal par fours, for the golf course you are playing. This will make the game of golf so much more fun, and give you a better idea of your handicap.

As a senior, it is very important to make sure you play your game and not be influenced by younger players, who may hit the ball much further. Remember, you can still score and beat other players who hit the ball longer than you do. Just stick with your natural swing that is inside you, and practice your short game.

A couple of years ago, the seniors in the next picture came through my golf academy. They had a marvelous time learning how to improve their games by trusting that their improvement depended upon their own innate abilities.

No matter your age, physical stature or current scoring average, you can improve and have fun doing it! No one forced them to put on those happy faces!

So if you don't currently have a professional golf instructor, now is the time to seek one out. When looking around for a good instructor, make sure you ask if they have a teaching program for seniors. Then jump in and get started on your journey of playing better golf and having fun.

A few years ago I ran a senior golf league. Although if you are familiar with senior leagues, I don't think any one person ever is the only one to make the decisions. Funny thing about when we get older, we somehow become very fixed in our ways and personalities.

There were anywhere from twenty-four to sixty senior golfers who played golf twice a week. The players were assigned the appropriate tee box, based on their abilities to hit the ball off the tee. There were some players in their late sixties and early seventies who still played the regular men's tees, while other younger players played the up tees. As I mentioned earlier, this made it more fun for the players to compete in their weekly competitions.

Here are a few things that, as we get older, can be a bit disconcerting on the golf course. As we lose our perfect hearing and eye sight, it is sometimes difficult to hear other players and follow the flight of our golf ball. If you experience either one of these difficulties, just be aware of it and don't be embarrassed to ask for another player to watch your ball or to speak up a little.

We also aren't as mobile as we once were. If you are paired with a player who has some difficulty walking briskly, be courteous and drive him to his ball, as close as you can, as often as you can. But please don't drive the player up on the tee box or the green. Believe it or not, I have seen that.

If you enjoy playing as a couple, there are senior couple leagues in almost every area of the country. Relaxing with couples with the same interests and age can be most rewarding. Check with your local golf professional and see if there is a league in your area.

As seniors, we also need to make sure we eat properly before and during a round of golf. Unless there is a medical reason not to, it is best if you have some fruit, nuts or some type of energy bar. It's probably a good idea before you play and at the turn after nine holes. Drink plenty of water and if you start to feel overheated, take a break and cool off immediately.

And finally, make sure you do the stretching exercises we have discussed. Go easy at first, but the more time you spend getting your body more flexible, the better you will play and the better you will feel the next day.

I'll leave you with this story. Just recently I had so much fun playing a recreational round of golf with some good senior friends. They are three fun and mad cap couples who are really enjoying life and golf.

It has become a tradition for the guys to play jokes on the gals. They will leave a golf ball in the hole, hide in the woods and run out and tee the ladies tee shot in the fairway...well you get the idea. One of the best was when the guys moved the ladies tee markers to the bulkhead. When the ladies arrived, needless to stay, they were confused at first, but soon realized that the guys would have had to be the guilty ones.

Here comes the fun part. The ladies are going to bet the guys that they can beat them on the number one handicap hole on my home course. So the ladies have asked me to help them get the guys the next time we play together.

Since there is little chance that they will read this before it happens, this is what we are going to do. I have arranged for men's and senior tee markers, just before we arrive at the tee, to be placed back with the pro tees on the most difficult hole on the course. I will of course replace the tee markers before I leave the tee box.

The ladies tees will be put at the junior tee box. This will make the hole a four hundred and eighty five yard par four hole for the guys and a two hundred and ten yard hole for the ladies. If the ladies win the hole with the lowest score, the men have to take them shopping.

Since the guys do not drive the ball long off the tee, this is very likely to do them in. I'll be playing with the guys and will inform them that the forward tee boxes are closed for renovations. It should be a lot of fun to see the guy's reactions.

What's the bottom line to all of this? You need to have fun on the course and whatever makes the most fun for you and your group, as long as you don't bother others, have a great time. Hope you had fun reminiscing with the fun pictures in this chapter!

NOTES

~~~~~~~~~~~~~~~~~~~~

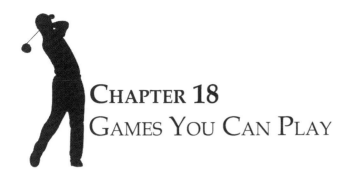

CHAPTER 18
GAMES YOU CAN PLAY

Games people play. Sound familiar? Well here are some fun games you can play with your golfing partners. Because there are so many different games, I have named just a few to give you an idea of some in case you've run out.

DIFFERENT FORMATS

Team handicap match: a, b, c, d players are paired together and play a best ball competition. Low net team wins!

Modified team handicap match where the players play a Texas scramble off every tee, then play their own ball thru hole out. A Texas scramble is when all players tee off and you use the best drive. You can also play this with your own tee ball on par threes!

Captain's choice with or without handicaps! A Captain's choice is when you use the best shot through hole out and all players play from the same best shot location.

Second shot Texas scramble: the best second shot is used instead of the drive. The players then use their own ball thru hole out.

Teams score the low gross on the par fours and the low net on the par threes and par fives!

Three sixes: team handicap match where the teams score the one low net ball on the first six holes, the low net two balls on the second six holes and the low net three balls on the third six holes. The low three balls is first place, low two balls second place, and low one ball is third place!

Two player scramble: players are blind drawn or paired and play a captain's choice with or without handicap!

Reverse sandlot: players are assigned as a, b, c, or d players. The d players are the captains and select their team taking turns selecting a 'c" then "b" and finally an "a" player. Teams then compete in a traditional captain and crew competition or any four player format!

Alternate shot: players are paired in twosomes and one player is assigned to tee off on the even number holes and the other player assigned the odd number holes, and then each player alternates shots until the ball is holed out.

No three putts: team handicap match where all second putts are good. So go for the gusto on every putt. The ball must be putted the first time from the putting surface!

Eighteen putts: as soon as the ball comes to rest on the putting surface the putt is good. This rewards players hitting the greens in regulation.

Round robin is when you have a threesome playing and you rotate a partner every six holes. You can play any type format.

The below great article is provided online by the [10]USGA.

The USGA, a proponent of promoting competitive fun play, offers information and hints for clubs interested in hosting their own events. From individual events to team competitions to season championships, the Association covers a myriad of ways clubs can sponsor competition.

Just as a steady diet of meat and potatoes loses its appeal over time, an endless routine of stroke-play rounds can dull a player's sense of competition and enjoyment. While the Rules of Golf cannot be applied to some of these games, especially when match play and stroke play are contested simultaneously, they can provide a diversion from a schedule of club championships and interclub and intra-club team matches. (For more standard forms of play and their recommended handicap allowances, please see Rules 29-32 and Appendix I in the Rules of Golf book or the USGA Handicap System Manual).

Early-Season Events

Get-Acquainted Tournament

Excellent for early in the season and for groups where new members are being introduced. Each player selects a partner with whom he has never played.

Four-ball stroke-play (better ball of partners) scoring; gross and net prizes may be awarded. (Men — 90% of Course Handicap; Women — 95% of Course Handicap)

Note: It is recommended that Committees consider it a condition of four-ball stroke-play competitions that the Course Handicaps of the members of a side may not differ by more than eight strokes. A side with a large difference between Course Handicaps has an advantage over a side with a small Course Handicap difference. If a difference of more than eight strokes cannot be avoided, it is suggested that an additional 10 percent reduction be applied to the Course Handicaps of the members of each side with a Course Handicap difference exceeding eight strokes.

Field Day

Useful for promoting interest in the club among prospective members. Each member invites three guests for the day, usually including dinner. Either best-ball-of-four (Men — 80% of Course Handicap; Women — 90% of Course Handicap) or two best-balls-of-four (Men — 90% of Course Handicap; Women — 95% of Course Handicap), stroke-play scoring; or individual scoring (full Course Handicaps) with separate prizes for best guest scores.

Individual Events

Nassau Tournament

Handicap stroke play event where handicap strokes are taken hole by hole as they fall on the score card and prizes are awarded for the best front nine, the best back nine and the best 18 holes. The advantage is that a player making a poor start, or tiring at the finish, may still win a prize for his play on the other nine.

Drop-Out Tournament

A variation on competing against par on a match-play basis. Each player is allowed his full Course Handicap, with strokes taken as designated on the score card. (For these games, it is helpful if the handicap strokes are indicated on the score card before the round.) The player then plays "against" par, remaining in the contest only until he loses a hole to par. The winner is the player going farthest around the course.

A variation of this game has each player in a "match" against par, the winner being the player most "up" on par, as if he had played a match-play competition (the winner may "beat" the course 4 and 3, for example). Both formats may be used for individuals or teams.

Flag Tournament

Each player is given a small flag, with his name on the flagstick. Using full Course Handicap, each player continues until he has used the number of strokes equaling par plus his Course Handicap. For example, a player with a Course Handicap of 14 playing a par-72 course would be allowed 86 strokes. When he has used his allotment of strokes, he plants his flag beside his ball. Prizes can be awarded to the players who plant their flags farthest around the course — playing extra holes beyond the 18th, if necessary — or to every player who holes out at the 18th green within his allotted number of strokes.

Kickers' Tournament

Good when accurate handicap information for a large percentage of players is not available. The Committee draws a number, advising players that the number is, for example, between 60 and 70. Players select their own "handicaps" without knowing the number drawn. The player whose "net score" equals, or is closest to, the number drawn, is the winner.

Throw-Out Tournament

Before returning their score cards, players are allowed to cross out a designated number of worst holes (for example, three holes). Course Handicaps usually are reduced in proportion to the number of holes rejected. The winner has the lowest score for the remaining holes.

Blind-Holes Tournament

Rewards steady play — and those with a little luck. After all players have left the first tee, a blind draw determines which nine holes of the 18 played will count toward everyone's total score — the other holes will be crossed out — so the players have no knowledge of which holes will count until they complete their rounds. One-half of Course Handicaps usually are used to compile net totals.

Most 3s, 4s and 5s

Players use full Course Handicap, taking strokes as designated on the score card. Prizes are awarded to the players scoring the most 3s, 4s and 5s.

Fewest Putts

Only strokes taken once the ball is on the putting green are counted. The winner is the player using the fewest number of "putts" for the round. No Course Handicaps used.

Syndicate Tournament

The field is divided into classes according to Course Handicaps: Class A may be players with handicaps of 7 and under; Class B, 8 to 15; Class C, 16 to 24, etc. (The Committee should determine these classes or use already-established handicap classes.) The player who makes the lowest score in his class on a hole wins a syndicate. Syndicates may be cumulative; in the event that one or more holes are tied, those syndicates go to the player next winning a hole. Each player pays an entry fee of one golf ball; the total balls in each class are divided by 18 to determine the value of a single syndicate, and each player's prize is determined by the number of syndicates he has won.

String Tournament

Each player or team is given a length of string, instead of handicap strokes. The string is measured out to allow one foot for each handicap stroke. The player (or team) may move his ball by hand to a more favorable spot at any time, at any place on the course (including on the putting green and into the hole), measuring with the string the distance the ball was moved and then cutting off the equivalent length of string. When the string is used up, the player (or team) is on his own.

Eclectic (Selected Score)

Each player plays 36 holes. From his two score cards, he selects his better score on each hole. The winner is the player with the lowest total score for the selected 18 holes. If net prizes are awarded, full Course Handicaps usually are used. This event may be completed in a day or extended over a weekend.

No Alibi Tournament

Instead of deducting handicap strokes where they are designated on the score card, each player is allowed to replay during the round the number of shots equal to three-quarters of his Course Handicap. A stroke replayed must be used even if it is worse than the original, and cannot be replayed a second time. The converse format (Replay Tournament) is also entertaining: each player has an opponent who can recall a given number of a player's best shots and ask that they be replayed.

Consolation Tournament

This event is held at the end of the season using any desired format. The only players eligible to compete, however, are those who did not win a tournament prize during the season. If desired, prizes may be given to every competitor.

Shoot-Out

Determine the number of holes involved, then assemble a group of players that is one higher (nine holes, 10 players; 18 holes, 19 players). Everyone plays the first hole, as a group, with the player making the highest score eliminated. Ties for the highest score are broken by "closest-to-the-hole" contests from around the putting green, including chip shots, pitch shots and bunker shots. Play continues on subsequent holes until only a survivor remains. If handicaps are used, strokes are taken as designated on the score card. Use percentages of Course Handicaps equal to the number of holes played.

Chicago System   Each player is given a point-quota, based on his Course Handicap. Points are scored: bogey-1; par-2; birdie-4; eagle-8. The player whose point total for 18 holes most exceeds his point-quota (or comes closest to it if no one exceeds it), wins. Find your point-

-quota opposite your Course Handicap in the table below.

Crse. Hcp.	Qta.	Crse. Hcp.	Qta.	Crse. Hcp.	Qta.	Crse. Hcp.	Qta.	Crse. Hcp.	Qta.	Crse. Hcp.	Qta.
1	38	7	32	13	26	19	20	25	14	31	8
2	37	8	31	14	25	20	19	26	13	32	7
3	36	9	30	15	24	21	18	27	12	33	6
4	35	10	29	16	23	22	17	28	11	34	5
5	34	11	28	17	22	23	16	29	10	35	4
6	33	12	27	18	21	24	15	30	9	36	3

Nutshell Championship

Sometimes called a "Miniature Championship" since it squeezes a single-elimination tournament into 36 holes. A nine-hole stroke-play qualifying round is held early in the morning. Qualifiers are divided into flights of eight, with the match-play draw based on qualifying scores as follows: 1 vs. 8; 4 vs. 5; 2 vs. 7; 3 vs. 6. All matches are then nine holes, first round before lunch, and last two rounds in the afternoon.

Approach and Putting Contest

Each contestant approaches and holes out three balls from 25, 50 and 100 yards off the putting green. Each ball should be played from a different direction. The winner is the one holing out all three balls in the fewest number of strokes.

Cross-Country

The course is not played in its usual order, instead tournament directions supplied to each player read something like this:

1st Hole: From 1st tee to 3rd green;

2nd Hole: From 4th tee to 10th green;

3rd Hole: From 11th tee to 7th green; etc.

The teeing ground for each hole should be near the putting green of the hole last played, to avoid long walks from green to tee. This type of event is often played once the season has ended.

Team Events

Scratch and Scramble Tournament

Play is four-ball stroke play. On each hole, partners' scores are added and divided by two to obtain the team's score. Play is more interesting if players with high and low handicaps are paired together. The handicap of each team is determined by taking a percentage of each partners' Course Handicap (Men — 90%; Women — 95%), adding them together and dividing by two.

Dot Tournament

Players are teamed as in four-ball match play. Each team is credited on each hole with one dot (a) for the longest drive in the fairway, (b) for hitting the first ball onto the putting green, (c) for having the closest ball to the hole on the approach shot, (d) for one-putting and (e) for the lowest score on the hole. The team having the most dots at the end of the 18 holes wins an appropriate token, usually in golf balls from the team with which it is paired.

Foursomes

This a standard Sunday afternoon feature at many clubs, and can be played in three ways. The "official way" is for the partners to alternate driving from each tee and then to play alternate shots until the ball is holed (Rule 29). (If handicaps are used, allow 50% of the partners' combined Course Handicaps). The game is perhaps more enjoyable for average golfers if both partners drive from each tee and select which ball to play thereafter. (If this format is used, allow 40% of the partners' combined Course Handicaps.) A third method was introduced by Mr. and Mrs. Richard Chapman with interesting results. The partners both drive from each tee, and then each plays a second shot with the other's ball. After the second shots, a choice is made regarding the ball with which the hole will be completed, alternate shots being continued until the ball is holed. (The player with the lower Course Handicap is allowed 60% of their Course Handicap. The player with the higher Course Handicap is allowed 40%)

Blind Partners

This is an 18-hole stroke play event using a percentage of Course Handicaps (Men - 90% of Course Handicap; Women - 95% of Course Handicap). Players may play with anyone of their choice. But partners are not drawn until the last group has teed off, so a player does not know his partner until he has finished. The winner is the team with the lowest better-ball score.

Scramble

Each team consists of four players. On each hole, each team member drives and the best drive is selected by the team captain. Each team member then plays a second shot from the spot where the selected drive lay and the best second shot is selected. This process is repeated until the hole is completed. There are variations on this event and often times certain restrictions imposed (i.e., each team members' drive must be used at least 3 times). For handicap purposes, it is fairest if each team consists of an A, B, C & D player (based on established handicap classes). The following percentages of Course Handicaps are used: A— 20%; B— 15%; C — 10%; D — 5%. If teams consist of just two players, the following percentages of Course Handicaps are used: A— 35%; B — 15%.

Season Events

Ringer Tournament

A player builds his eighteen-hole total over the season by posting his lowest score on each hole. Scoring is on a gross basis.

Round Robin Tournament

Each entrant plays a handicap match against every other entrant during the season; allowing the full difference between Course Handicaps in each match. A time limit usually is set for completion of each round; a player who cannot meet an opponent within the time limit forfeits the match, but may continue in the tournament. The winner is the player winning the most matches. (This season-long tournament could also be conducted in a team format at four-ball match play.)

Ladder Tournament

The names of all players are listed in order, according to either Course Handicaps or Handicap Indexes, at the start of the season. (Those players with the same Course Handicap are listed according to their Handicap Indexes. Players with the same Handicap Index are listed by the totals of their handicap differentials). A player may challenge any one of the three players immediately above to an 18-hole match. If the challenger wins, the players exchange places. If the challenger loses, that player may not challenge again until defending his own position against a challenger from below. Play is usually without handicaps.

Goat Tournament

Each member of the club is given an inexpensive token in the form of a goat, with his name on the reverse side. Any player may then challenge another to a handicap match, the winner to get the loser's "goat." After a player has lost his "goat," he may continue to challenge in an attempt to get another player's "goat." However, if he should lose and not have a "goat" with which to pay, he must purchase a "kid" for a nominal amount from the golf professional and give up the "kid." The "kid" is convertible into merchandise in the golf professional's shop. Only players with "goats" in their possession may be challenged, and players usually are not required to accept a challenge more often than once a week. Records of "goat" play and the current location of each "goat" usually are posted so that a player may know who has his "goat" and who has the most "goats." The winner is the player holding the most "goats" at the end of the season.

Pro vs. Members

The golf professional agrees to play a handicap match against each member as he is challenged, making a nominal charge for each round. The professional plays at scratch. The member making the best showing in his match receives a prize from the golf professional at the end of the season.

[10]USGA, Farhills, New Jersey

-End of Article-

And finally, here is a tournament system you can use if your players do not have established handicaps.

EXPLAINING THE CALLAWAY SYSTEM
How to Use the Callaway Scoring System When Official Handicaps are Unavailable

The Callaway System (or Callaway Scoring System) is a sort of 1-day handicapping system that can be used in events where most of the golfers do not have real handicap indexes.

For example, at a company outing, most of the golfers may not carry official handicap indexes. How can they all - with widely different playing abilities - compete fairly at stroke play? The Callaway System allows a "handicap allowance" to be determined and then applied to each golfer's score.

When the Callaway System is in use, all competitors tee off and play stroke play, scoring in the normal fashion with one exception - double par is the maximum score on any given hole (i.e., on a par 4, 8 is the maximum score).

Following the round, gross scores are tallied. Based on each golfer's gross score (using the double par maximum), each golfer tallies up a prescribed number of worst scores from their scorecard, then applies a second adjustment that may add or subtract additional strokes.

The result is a total that is something similar to a net score using real handicaps.

A couple points:

• The higher a competitor's gross score, the more holes that player will be deducting;
• Holes deducted begin with the highest score; if a player gets to deduct one hole and his highest score is an 8, then an 8 is what gets deducted;

• Holes deducted begin with the highest score; if a player gets to deduct one hole and his highest score is an 8, then an 8 is what gets deducted;

• Scores on the 17th and 18th holes may not be deducted, even if one (or both) of them are the competitor's highest score.

• Even after high scores are added together for the allowance, the second adjustment must be made; this adjustment might add or subtract 2, 1 or 0 strokes from a players Callaway handicap.

• Once the appropriate number of high scores has been tallied, and the second adjustment is made, the player is left with a net score.

Sounds complicated, eh? That's why the Callaway System comes complete with a handy reference chart.

The chart below should make things much easier to grasp. Look over the chart, then look below the chart for an example.

Gross (using double par max.)					Handicap Deduction
		70	71	72	Scratch
73	74	75			1/2 of Worst Hole
76	77	78	79	80	Worst Hole
81	82	83	84	85	1 1/2 Worst Holes
86	87	88	89	90	2 Worst Holes
91	92	93	94	95	2 1/2 Worst Holes
96	97	98	99	100	3 Worst Holes
101	102	103	104	105	3 1/2 Worst Holes
106	107	108	109	110	4 Worst Holes
111	112	113	114	115	4 1/2 Worst Holes
116	117	118	119	120	5 Worst Holes
121	122	123	124	125	5 1/2 Worst Holes
126	127	128	129	130	6 Worst Holes
-2	-1	0	+1	+2	**Handicap Adjustment**

Before our examples, a couple notes about the chart: This chart applies to a par-72 course. If par is different, simply add or subtract the number of strokes - corresponding to the difference in par - from the Gross Scores. For example, if par is 71, then subtract 1 from each of the Gross Scores listed above. Also, half scores are rounded up. If a player is deducting half of 7, then that 3.5 is rounded up to 4. And finally, the maximum a golfer can deduct under the Callaway System is 50 strokes. OK, an example of the Callaway System in action:

Tiger shoots 64. No deductions or adjustments are made because Tiger's score is lower than the scores listed on the chart. Vijay shoots 71, which is on the chart and the column to the right ("Handicap Deduction") shows that a player shooting 71 plays at scratch - no adjustments.

The Golf Guide, however, shoots 97. Find 97 in the chart above and we see that its row (going across) corresponds to a handicap deduction of "3 Worst Holes". So the Golf Guide finds the three worst holes on his scorecard. The Golf Guide's three worst holes are a 9, an 8 and a 7. Total those up and we get a handicap deduction of 24. Now we apply the second adjustment. Go back to 97 in the chart above; follow the column down to the "handicap adjustment" on the bottom line. The column for 97 corresponds to a handicap adjustment of -1. That means we're going to subtract a stroke from our handicap deduction of 24. So our final, adjusted handicap allowance is 23.

And our net Callaway System score is 97 minus 23, or 74. So using the chart is a matter of finding the gross score, looking across the row for the handicap deduction, then looking down the column for the adjustment.

NOTES

~~~~~~~~~~~~~~~~~~~~~~

CHAPTER **19**
NINETEENTH HOLE

After a satisfying round of golf, most golfers head to what is commonly referred to as "the Nineteenth Hole". For some golfers it is in the clubhouse, while for others it is a local food and beverage establishment. Whatever your preference, most golfers join the guys and/or gals after play for food, drinks and camaraderie.

This is where golf bragging excels, war stories unfold, world problems are solved, religion is debated, sports are watched on TV, recipes are exchanged, drink mixes are recommended, beers are guzzled, shots are downed, bar food is engulfed like there's no tomorrow, golf tips are given (wanted by the recipient or not), great buys are emotionally recited, cars and trucks are debated, trivia is played, music is enjoyed, medical problems are discussed, spousal disputes are resolved/or not, weather is talked about with great authority, TV shows are argued about, bartenders become: your best friend, psychologist, monk, rabbi, minister, doctor, marriage counselor, and most importantly, your server of alcohols.

Yes, just about every topic you can imagine has an expert on the subject. Some even say the only reason they play golf is for the camaraderie at the nineteenth hole.

So, I thought it only fitting that some of these stories are repeated here in this book, in no particular order, to make it even more fun.

Did you know that the reported lowest score for eighteen holes on a regulation golf course is a fifty-five? Yep, in nineteen thirty-six, an English Professional shot a fifteen under par round, which by all reports, still stands as the record. Now you have a goal to go after!

Did you know that only Tiger Woods has been the defending champion, at the same time, for all four of the majors? He failed to do it in the same year, but had all four trophies on his mantel at the same time.

Several years ago, two of my buddies and I were having a few cocktails at a local bar. It was a very nice place, with an extremely fine decor. How the "one-up-man-ship" got started, I do not remember. But somehow we were coming up with shots and drinks that were just plain "knock you on your seat" type drinks.

Well, I made a bet with Mr. D that he could not handle a rusty nail. For those of you who are unfamiliar with this drink, it is two alcoholic beverages consisting of a liqueur, Drambuie, and a Scotch Whiskey. Mr. D was primarily a beer drinker, and had already had his fair share. The bartender served him the drink in a short glass and before I knew it, Mr. D had downed the entire drink. He told the bartender he would have another. I told him it was a sipping type drink, not a shot. Didn't matter to him, he slammed two more of them.

My next bet with him was that he would not be able to walk down the hall as we left. Of course, we were not letting him drive and had his keys. Well he bounced off both walls, knocking over artificial palm trees as he went.

What was amazing is that he was still able to talk pretty well, but I won the second bet, *and it was an interesting ride home*!

For those of you, who like flame and a knockout shot, give a "Green Lizard" a go. It consists of Green Chartreuse, a rare liqueur made by monks, and Rum One-Fifty-One. Light it on fire, extinguish it and down it. You do not want to sip this drink, as it tastes like gasoline. It will, however, light your fire! Not too many people survive upright with more than a couple!

For you gentlemen who would like to take care of your lady's beverage desires, here are three drinks they are bound to be impressed with. First is the "Between the Sheets". I know, sounds like something you would only find in a bar. However, it is said to have been invented in Jerusalem as an after dinner drink. It is three quarters of an ounce each of Cognac, Light Rum, Cointreau, and one half ounce of lemon juice. If your lady is a Gin drinker, mix equal parts of Cognac, Cointreau, and Dry Gin. This version is not as sweet.

The second one is a "Night Cap". Mix two ounces of Light Rum, one teaspoon powdered sugar, warm milk and sprinkle with Nutmeg. The third one is from the beauty salon, called a "Platinum Blonde". My lady loves this drink! Mix two ounces Vodka, one ounce Coconut Rum, one and one half ounce pineapple juice, one half ounce soda water, one half ounce seven up and garnish with a Maraschino cherry. Your lady will love it too!

Remember, always drink responsibly!

Ladies, want to serve your man food he will love, and love you even more for cooking? Popeye and all guys love this one. "A Man's Spinach Dip". Brown one pound each of ground beef and your favorite sausage, add one chopped onion, two pounds Velveeta cheese, one can green chilies and tomatoes, one can mushroom soup and one teaspoon garlic powder and serve hot with your favorite dipping chips.

You'll be a heroine! And… it's perfect for getting him to watch the football game with you instead of going to a sports bar! You may have one problem though; the recipe makes enough to have his buddies over for the game.

If your man has a sweet tooth, this one will make him as sweet as the dessert. ("Banana Le`Orange"-Lumpy's special recipe). It's easy to make and absolutely something you would find in the finest restaurants in the world.

In a skillet, pour two ounces of Grand Marnier, add two bananas cut into one half inch rounds, add two tablespoons brown sugar, one quarter teaspoon of cinnamon, and a quarter cup of cream cheese fruit dip. Serve hot over vanilla ice cream. You can substitute pears if he is not a banana lover.

Here's a funny story. While playing golf at a nice golf course years ago, I witnessed one of the most unusual events you will see on a golf course. Several groups of golfers were enjoying a relaxing lunch and I was seated by the window with a great view of the golf course. Just as I glanced out the window, I saw a golf cart take off down a hill with no driver, with a man and a woman running after it. The man jumped in the cart and got it stopped just as it was about to plunge into a lake.

Now comes the best part. The couple got into an argument, probably about who didn't set the brake properly. The man drove the cart, as fast as it would go. I think he thought he was operating a locomotive. He drove up past where it had been parked, and started down the next hill. All of a sudden he hit a big bump, and the woman went flying out of the cart, landed on her rump, and rolled down to the bottom of the hill, at about the same time as the man arrived with the cart.

As the man hopped out of the cart to go to her aid, without missing a beat, she jumped up, went over to the cart, unbuckled the man's golf bag, and drove the cart away up towards the clubhouse. The man stood there dumbfounded looking at his bag lying on the ground. He shook his head, picked up his golf bag, and walked to the next hole.

Several of us went outside to watch what the lady was going to do. She drove the cart to the rear of a car, popped the trunk, threw her clubs in the car and sped away. Well, we found out from the General Manager that they always rode together and he mused as to how the golfer would get home. I'm not sure there is any moral here; I will let you draw your own conclusions.

Speaking of a lake, we have all heard the story about a guy who throws his clubs in a lake after hitting more than one ball in the water. He walks back to the parking lot, only to discover that his keys and wallet were in his bag. He, of course, must return to the lake, jump in, and retrieve his possessions.

Well, while working at a golf course in my mid twenties, I was out putting ice in the water jugs. Number nine returned to the clubhouse and the tee shot was over a lake. Had I not witnessed this myself, I would not have believed it. After this golfer hit all the golf balls he had in his bag into the water, he drove to the edge of the hazard and stopped. He yelled, "You have all my balls, you might as well have the bag and clubs," as he heaved them into the lake.

That day was a Saturday, and three Saturdays later he came into the pro shop and purchased all new equipment. I asked him what made him decide to play golf again and buy all new equipment. He said his wife could not take his company anymore, and gave him eight hundred dollars to go buy new equipment so he would not be in the house on Saturday and Sunday any more! Hope this doesn't sound familiar to any of you.

We all dream of being a great golfer. At the nineteenth hole, *no one can steal your dream.* We can tell the best and most convincing stories of what great shots we played. Granted, it may have only been one in the round, but in our minds, it was the entire round that we dreamt was great!

Don't let anyone steal your dream of playing great golf.

Each of us may define greatness differently, but that's what makes golf such a great sport. So go ahead…play for the dream.

NOTES

~~~~~~~~~~~~~~~~~~~~~

CHAPTER 20
SUMMARY

What a journey we have taken together in "The Spiritual Golfer". I have defined greatness by categories and you have chosen the category you most likely fit into. Based upon this, you have learned how to find the natural swing inside you, which lies deep within your spirit, how to bring it out, and the subsequent greatness. I have tried to make the journey fun and uncomplicated, but detailed enough so not only can the established player take something away that will help them, but still allow the beginner to understand the golf swing. Thank you for taking this journey with me. It is my fondest wish that you have discovered that natural swing inside your spirit.

My editor and I had quite a discussion about what to include in the summary. However, together we concluded that it would be good for you, the reader, to have a highlight of each chapter. This became difficult for me to do in some cases, because a lot of what we have covered requires an all encompassing explanation. With that in mind, however, let us finish our journey together in a review of: "The Spiritual Golfer".

(Chapter One) *The great players have learned not to fight the natural swing inside them.* You have learned how to find the natural golf swing inside you, by first going back to the shot you hit in disgust. You see what happened was that you gave no thought as to how to hit that shot. You just swung. This is worth repeating; you gave no thought as to how to hit the shot and just swung. This naturally created another phenomenon. You also gave no thought to the results!

You learned one of the secrets of the great golfers. They conquer the fear of hitting a bad shot. They knock fear out! That is exactly what you did when you threw the ball down and just swung.

(Chapter Two) Next we examined the second mental aspect of the game that great players master. The great players accept whatever the environment is as a natural occurring event. They welcome and enjoy it. The examination of what physically occurs on the first tee revealed that instead of just swinging like you do at the pine cone, you change to trying to hit the ball and make the shot that you desire. You discovered that the environment with your playing partners was not accepted. You learned how to succeed by getting this ingrained in your mind forever and ever. Just brush the grass and '**The ball simply gets in the way of the swing**'. Just as the pine cone got in the way of your swing when you warmed up, that is exactly the way you want to swing when you make a pass with the ball in the way.

The proper swing positions were introduced in order to learn how to get the proper timing, rhythm, and tempo.

You learned that you must accept the fact that you remember by pictures. To prove this, if I ask you what an elephant is, what is the first thing that comes into your mind? That's right, you picture an elephant.

So when I say what a perfectly smooth golf swing looks like, you probably picture Ernie Els, Fred Couples, Davis Love III, or other players from our golf history such as Bobby Jones, Sam Snead or Payne Stewart. If you have another favorite, that is fine too.

The important thing is to find one of the great swingers of the golf club and learn all you can by watching what they do. When you practice your golf swing, it is important to try and feel like they look in your minds' eye. Not that I consider myself in the league of these great players, but I provided the stop action photos of my swing to help give you the mental images.

You have learned that it is necessary to clear your mind of all clutter so you can relax and enjoy playing your round of golf.

You learned the three things that great players have learned to do. They trust their golf swings, accept their environment and use their natural timing, rhythm and tempo.

Within "trust your golf swing" is focusing on the swing and not the mechanics of how to make the swing as well as being confident that your swing is going to work, thus the word trust. Failure to believe that the swing will create the shot you have in mind is the same as not trusting.

Within the "environment acceptance" is also blocking out any unwanted distractions.

Within "timing, rhythm and tempo" is the act of swinging too hard or trying a swing that you have not gained total confidence in.

(Chapter Three) The great players' three physical things they have in common were outlined. First and most importantly is the impact position. The left side (right side if a lefty) always arrives at the ball first and the club head does not pass the hands at impact with the ball. Second, they maintain the triangle from address through the impact zone. Third, they maintain their balance which is evident in their finish.

We studied the proper swing positions in depth. You learned not to throw the club from the top, commonly called casting like in fishing.

You learned that the most important position to master is the impact position and that flipping the club to hit the ball is a horrible position and rarely results in a good shot. It would be a good idea to take the time to review this chapter and study the correct positions.

(Chapter Four) In order to strike good golf shots we took an in-depth view of the inside path golf swing. It is vitally important to strike the ball from the inside with your hands rolling and releasing through impact.

To accomplish this, my assigned drill was to swing in my back yard until I created "half moon shape" type semi-divots in the grass. In other words, mow the grass with my five-wood. You will recall that it took me about thirty days or so.

(Chapter Five) In chapter five we covered the swing faults that most amateur golfers have. These faults can cause a myriad of golf shots. The swing faults are: swinging too upright on the backswing, keeping their feet pointed straight, throwing the club from the top, a reverse weight transfer, failing to roll the hands at impact, swinging outside to in, flipping the club at impact, and not releasing the club.

We covered how to correct each of the swing faults and particularly the failure to roll the hands at impact. Failing to roll the hands at impact can cause a slice or fade even if you have the correct swing path. Leaving the club face open is the result and it adds loft to the club. After the ball is struck, it is going to the right. If the path was correct the ball starts to the right and turns to the right. If the path was outside then the ball starts to the left and slices back to the right.

To properly understand the rolling of the hands, visualize the back of the left hand rolling down to the ground as you swing through the ball. The baseball swing is also a great drill because almost all golfers naturally roll their hands when swinging at chest level.

We took a look at the smash factor. Simply put, the ball must be struck from the inside, on the sweet spot in order to gain the most distance. It is true that a slower swing speed striking the ball on the sweet spot of the club face will make the ball travel further than a faster swing hit in the heel or on the toe.

You discovered that it all comes back to your own natural swing that's inside you. You use the natural timing, rhythm and tempo, along with how fast you can swing on the correct path while still maintaining your balance.

Understand also that the entire golf swing only takes about two seconds! The moment of impact is only two tenths of one of those seconds. Do you really think in two tenths of a second that we can consciously control that release of speed that we have generated? Of course not; but we can interfere with its natural path and timing, by trying to control it. So don't try to hit the ball, *just brush the grass and let the ball get in the way*!

(Chapter Six) The grip pressure that is utilized is no more than necessary to hang on to the club and not throw the club when you swing. If you were holding a baby bird, you would not exert enough pressure to harm the little fella.

The most expedient way I have found to explain how to relate the gripping of the golf club is to "shake hands with the grip". The grip is placed across the left hand at a diagonal. It is not placed in the fingers or the palm, but rather as a combination of both.

The club is gripped with the last three fingers of the left hand. The index finger wraps around the club and touches the thumb creating a sort of pincher. However, the index finger and thumb do not grip the club, but rest comfortably on the club to lend support.

The right hand grip is also held behind the meat of the hand. The two middle fingers of the right hand are all that grips the club. The little finger is either placed over the index finger of the left hand for an overlap grip or is placed between the index finger and the middle finger for an interlocking grip.

There are basically three types of grips: The ten finger grip, the interlock, and the overlap grip. Whichever grip you choose, the "V's" that form between the thumb and hand should both point somewhere between the chin and the right shoulder.

(Chapter Seven) In chapter seven we covered the specialty shots. These shots, when practiced, can lower your score. This is one of the areas that is difficult to highlight because each shot is explained in detail.

I think it best if you simply refer to the chapter for the particular shot you are seeking to learn. We covered the following specialty shots: uphill, downhill, side hill, fairway bunker, greenside bunker, hard pan, roots, pine straw, fifty yard bunker shot, left handed shot and how to draw and fade the ball.

(Chapter Eight) You learned the importance of properly fitted clubs and that it is certified professional club builders and/or certified professional club fitters who you want to seek out. With today's technology in the manufacturing of club heads, grips and shafts, I have yet to see a golfer, who, with the proper clubs and fitting, did not improve their ability to play golf.

(Chapter Nine) Discovering how to hit it further and physical fitness is a revealing chapter. There has probably never been a golfer who hasn't wanted to learn to hit the ball further. We took a scientific and natural look into this fascinating subject. I provided some insights from other view points so you could apply what you feel will help you in understanding how to hit the ball further. Take some time to review all this information that was provided.

(Chapter Ten) There is, of course, an important element to all that you have learned. That is practice. Practicing is an important part of excelling at anything you choose to do, especially sports. There are specific things you need to do to get the most out of practice. Knowing what, how and the time to spend on each area is crucial to getting the most out of your practice time.

The saying practice makes perfect is really correct when rephrased to "perfect practice makes perfect". So it does no good to practice the incorrect swing techniques. All you accomplish is engraining bad habits. The longer you teach your muscles to remember how not to do it correctly, the longer it is going to take to make the changes that allow you to make the natural golf swing that is inside you.

Putting is at the top of the list when it comes to practicing. With only having thirty-two putts, which is more than forty-four percent of your score of seventy-two, while your driver is only about nineteen percent. Wow, you probably just never thought about it this way before.

Learning how to find your dominate eye and how to line up properly, not just for putting, but for all shots, is crucially important. The greatest archer in the world cannot hit a target he is not aimed at.

If you are going to spend sixty minutes a day practicing, then you want to spend twenty minutes of that time on putting. Yes, it is that important. Make sure you spend quality time in all you're practicing.

(Chapter Eleven) While I go into detail on course management, there are three rules that should *never* be violated. The first is that when in trouble, get out safely. The second one is never to try a golf shot on the course that you have not practiced completely and fully. And, third, if a layup is called for, make sure you layup with plenty of room to spare.

(Chapter Twelve) Proper etiquette on the golf course is seldom taught, yet it defines who we are with our playing partners. For the most part, etiquette is just being polite and courteous. Take the time to read, in its entirety, what the USGA[17] has to say about etiquette in golf. It is Section I in the rules of golf. Below is the introduction:

This section provides guidelines on the manner in which the game of golf should be played. If they are followed, all players will gain maximum enjoyment from the game. The overriding principle is that consideration should be shown to others on the course at all times.

Golf is played, for the most part, without the supervision of a referee or umpire. The game relies on the integrity of the individual to show consideration for other players and to abide by the rules. All players should conduct themselves in a disciplined manner, demonstrating courtesy and sportsmanship at all times, irrespective of how competitive they may be. This is the spirit of the game of golf.

(Chapter Thirteen) Every golfer needs to pick up a rule book on the game of golf. However, I covered some of the rules that you commonly come across in a normal round of golf. Some of the rules covered are: ball on the cart path, lifting and marking a ball, embedded ball, tending the flagstick, water hazards, loose impediments, ball resting on green and fringe, giving advice to other players and slow play.

(Chapter Fourteen) Unfortunately, the only way you get experience in competitive golf is to play. However, there are certain things you can do to prepare yourself for competition.

First, get with and stay with an instructor that you believe in and trust. Make sure you find an instructor that understands playing and competing under pressure.

After awhile, the instructor will begin to learn your tendencies and know your swing. This is very important because you cannot see your own swing, but staying with the same instructor makes it easier for him to help you.

Taking lessons on a regular basis also gives you confidence in your swing and a support system. When you are competing it is easy to lose your confidence, but with the comforting words from your instructor in your head, you are more easily able to stay focused.

(Chapter Fifteen) When it comes to junior golf, all you parents and grandparents just need to remember that golf is a game. If you try to make your kids/grandkids develop too quickly, it can be very harmful to their mental and physical success in golf.

Now this does not mean to avoid encouraging them to do their best; simply allow them the same growth opportunities you allow them in other areas.

(Chapter Sixteen) Physically men and women are built differently. Now there's a big surprise, huh? In my opinion too much is made of the differences. There are, however, two swing faults I often see that are common to ladies, including my own beautiful lady. On the backswing, rather than turning their shoulders, ladies have a tendency to turn just enough to allow them to lift their arms up almost immediately. The second common swing fault is rather than a rotation of the hips, the hips are tilted laterally causing the loss of posture and a myriad of other swing problems.

(Chapter Seventeen) My fellow seniors, we had fun finding out what exactly defines the age of a senior. We know in golf it has been defined by the professional tour as fifty years of age. Just recently a dating service advertized "if you're 40 and would like to meet other seniors..." Social Security begins at age sixty-two. Others say it is when your junk mail contains a membership offer from AARP. Still others contend that if you're a baby boomer *you are* a senior.

However you define it, I hope you enjoyed the nostalgic trip with the pictures. Hopefully it brought back some fond memories.

(Chapter Eighteen) When it comes to golf, just as a steady diet of meat and potatoes loses its appeal over time, an endless routine of stroke-play rounds can dull a player's sense of competition and enjoyment. While the Rules of Golf cannot be applied to some of these games, especially when match play and stroke play are contested simultaneously, they can provide a diversion from a schedule of club championships and interclub and intra-club team matches.

So the USGA and I have provided you with some fun and different games you can play.

NOTES

~~~~~~~~~~~~~~~~~~~~

ACKNOWLEDGEMENTS

Tim Gillis, Producer, Entertainer - timgillisband.com
Big Joe Kriznuski, Author's former professional teacher
Tom Furgason, Author's former professional teacher
Debroy Mears, Author's Certifying Professional
Black Bear Golf Course, Longs, SC
Patrick Wilkerson, G. M., Black Bear Golf Club
Don Barnes, sunbeltseniorgolftour.com
Alvin Cloyd, Master Club Builder
John Robinson, Professional Instructor
Mike Schroeder, Professional Instructor
Getaway Golf Academy, Lady Amateurs
Dave Rago, Partner Fantasy Golf
Mike and Joann Chilson, Amateurs
George DePolo, Judge
Chad Eskew, Amateur
Danny Hynes, Amateur
Richard Hubbell, Amateur
Ray Tommer, Amateur
Tom Gacioch, Amateur
Joe Kustron., Amateur
Warren Thebolt, Amateur
Robert Gamble, Amateur
John Munley, Amateur
Steve Leghart, Amateur
Jim McCready, Amateur
Hawk Finnemore, Amateur
Dave "The Fighter", Amateur
Robert Hovell, Amateur
Steve Eddy, Amateur
Kevin Meyers, Amateur
Steve Pratt, Allover Media
Mark Eiken, Allover Media
Scott, Parks and Recreation
Pictured Getaway Golf Academy Graduates:
Charles "Barney" Gibbons
Barbara "Barb" Gibbons
Irene "Rennie" Johnston
Gary Player, Golf Ambassador, Tour Player, Golf Legend

Special Family Acknowledgements

Sara, Stephanie, Vic, Mike, Audrey, Mason, Eli, Will, Henry, Coralee

Dedicated to "Beth", Author's Beautiful Lady

I would like to give a special thank you to all the Professional Golfers who taught at the Fantasy Golf Camps over the years, whom I have had the great pleasure to not only learn from and play golf with, but observe their teaching techniques as well.

Tom Kite
Davis Love III
Lanny Wadkins
Curtis Strange
Peter Jacobsen
Gary Koch
Al Geiberger
Payne Stewart
John Daly
Peter Persons
Robert Wrenn
Art Sellinger
Steve Pate
Fuzzy Zoeller
Curt Byrum
Dudley Hart
Mark Carnevale
Mike Standly
Scott Davenport
Howard Twitty
Blaine McCallister
Chris Johnson
Ed Dougherty
I missed the camp with:
Jay Haas
Fred Funk

About The Author, Robert Lumpkin

Now resides in South Carolina with his beautiful lady Jeanne. Has two daughters and six grandchildren. Started playing golf on the high school team at age sixteen, some forty-three years ago. Began playing professional golf at age thirty-two, and later opened his own golf range and began teaching golf. Spanning those years, he has been involved in nearly all aspects of the game, but his true love is teaching.

Certified Professional Golf Instructor

Certified Professional Club Builder

Certified Professional Club Fitter

Certified Trainer for Instructors and Club Builders

Founder and Director of Golf / Getaway Golf Academy

Professional Golf Consultant / Expert Court Witness

Former Chairman / Fantasy Golf International LLC (Fantasy Golf Camp)

Former Professional Mini -Tour Player

Tournament Organization Director

Public Speaker

Contributing Writer / Author / Illustrator

Other Published Books: "Patriots Among Us: Never Forget"

A suspenseful thriller

Hobbies: Pencil Artist / Gourmet Chef

Author's Contact Information:

Golf email: lumpysgolf@yahoo.com
Facebook: R. D. Lumpkin
Twitter: rdlumpkinauthor
Patriots email: author@patriotsamongus.com
Web site: www.patriotsamongus.com

FOR LESSONS WITH LUMPY

Mr. Lumpkin is the Founder and Director of Golf of the Getaway Golf Academy, located at Black Bear Golf Club in Longs, SC. Conveniently just twenty minutes from Myrtle Beach, and fifteen minutes to the beautiful Atlantic Ocean beaches.

The Club offers golfers a round as it was meant to be…a true classic parkland course completely engulfed by nature and enhanced by 23 beautiful finger lakes. Designed by Tom Jackson, the course itself will force you to use every club in your bag and the wide fairways instill confidence for the meek and forgiveness for the bold. Stay at a nearby hotel tucked away in the outskirts of Myrtle Beach, yet easily accessible to major attractions, restaurants, theatres, entertainment, shopping and of course…beaches. The New Carolina Bays Parkway (Route 31) has made Little River and Longs the perfect place to get away from it all while enjoying the quiet and convenience of the secluded waterways. Hotels offer spectacular intercostals waterway views and waterfront dining. Moderately priced, one to five day golf schools can be booked year round. Email: lumpysgolf@yahoo.com or contact America's Favorite Golf Schools at www.afgs.com and then select location: South Carolina - Little River.

THE SPIRITUAL GOLFER

WWW.THESPIRITUALGOLFER.COM

Made in the USA
Charleston, SC
06 April 2014